✞

BRENDAN MCGUIRE

God Bless

Fr. Brendan

the Weaving Divine Thread

Cycle A

authorHOUSE®

AuthorHouse™
1663 Liberty Drive
Bloomington, IN 47403
www.authorhouse.com
Phone: 1 (800) 839-8640

Published by AuthorHouse 12/06/2019

ISBN: 978-1-7283-3779-1 (sc)
ISBN: 978-1-7283-3780-7 (hc)
ISBN: 978-1-7283-3793-7 (e)

Library of Congress Control Number: 2019919551

Contents

Dedication

This book is dedicated to the *parishioners of Holy Spirit Parish, San Jose*. For the last 16 years I have been pastor of this wonderful community and they have inspired me to preach honestly about our faith and they have challenged me to be a disciple in the modern world. Thank you for your witness of faith especially in the difficult times.

As part of the process of developing the right message in the homily each week I share my "raw ideas" with some friends. For the last many years, one of those friends and parishioner, Jed De Torres has listened patiently, critiqued gently and reacted strongly to my ideas. Once again, I wish to express my gratitude to him for his patience, kindness and inspiration; his wisdom is now embedded in these homilies.

In a special way I want to acknowledge Frank Ricchio, who spent endless hours editing and proofing the texts of these homilies. Without his help this book would not have been a reality. The artwork for the cover of this book was created by Alex and Amber Vo. I thank them for their continued support of me and the parish. I also want to thank Penny Warne and all staff of Holy Spirit Parish in San Jose, California for their support over the many years. I also want to thank Mary Smith who has transcribed my homilies for many years and enabled me to publish my homilies weekly via email and the parish website.

Finally, I want to thank my brother Paul and his wife Maria and their family and my brother Vivian and his wife Kim and their family. They are the source of great love and truly the source of inspiration for so many homilies. Their friendship and love sustain me from week to week especially in this last difficult year in our Church. Thank you.

Acknowledgements

I am very grateful to the authors, editors and publishers of the following resources which have been inspirational to me and on which I have drawn in the course of preparing this book. I strongly recommend them to readers: *Celebration: An Ecumenical Worship Resource*, (Kansas City, Missouri: National Catholic Reporter Company, Inc.); *Connections*, (MediaWorks Londonderry, NH); *Homily Helps*, (St. Anthony Messenger Press: Cincinnati, OH); Catholic Digest, May 2008; Robert Waznak, S.S., *Like Fresh Bread*, (Mahwah, New Jersey: Paulist Press, 1993); Jeffrey Kluger, Mercury News, *Science of Simplexity Explains WWI Traffic* (Editorial, August 21, 2008).

Introduction

I truly believe that God is present to us every minute of every day. Yet we struggle to see or feel his presence. It seems to be that our modern lifestyle, with its busyness and instant access to so much information of the internet, makes it even more difficult to see and experience God in our lives. We are in constant "over stimulation" mode bombarded by so many sounds and noises each distracting us from seeing God in our lives. Coming to Church each Sunday affords us the opportunity to tune out the noise of the world and allow God to speak to the human heart.

It is the role of the priest and preacher to connect God's word to the daily life of the hearer of the Word at Mass. Most times my homily starts with a story that breaks open the scripture readings. Often the story is an experience of lived faith that I witness during the week. Then I connect it to God's story and hear some challenge from God for all of us to live throughout the week ahead.

I believe that God's ways are mysterious yet knowable, hidden yet understandable, and divine yet human. But we need to take the time to listen to him speak through the daily events of our lives. We need to stand back a little from our daily life to see the "pattern" that God is weaving through our lives.

The title of this book was inspired by the tapestries from the Cathedral of Angels in Los Angeles by artist John Nava. The tapestries are the largest collection hanging in a Catholic place of worship in the United States. Nava combined digital imaging and "Old Master" methods in creating the saints for the tapestries. He weaved the tapestry *Communion of Saints* consisting of females and males of all ages, races, occupations and vocations the world over. Saints from the Renaissance are intermingled with people from the 1st century and the 20th century. This was my inspiration for the name of the book as I believe when I preach, I am threading the Word of God intermingling it with the stories of people's lives from centuries past and to the 21st century.

My hope is that the woven stories here will help you to find a place in your soul to weave the Word of God and to trust that the Lord is weaving a divine story deep within you.

Are You Happy?

I was recently at my brother's house for dinner and we were engrossed in a normal conversation when their youngest boy, Sean, who was nearly 3 years old, started to pull at my leg. "Oncol Bridan, Oncol Bridan!", he exclaimed. He was so persistent we had to stop our conversation and ask, "Yes Sean, what?" He looked straight into my eyes and asked, "Are you happy, Oncol Bridan?" I was so startled by the question; I was really thrown off guard. "Am I happy, Sean?" I said in reply. And he repeats it again, as if it was a new mantra. "Are you happy, Oncol Bridan?" Of course, I got down on my knees and said, "Yes Sean, I am very happy." He smiled widely and asked the same thing to my brother and every other person who came into the house. The question threw me off since I was not expecting it.

That's the very thing that happens in today's Gospel and scripture readings. The Lord asks, "Are you ready?" Are you ready to meet your Maker, the Lord God? It's a sharp and pointed question and it's not for the light-hearted. And so, we ask it as we begin a new year for the Church. We celebrate Advent, a time of waiting and preparation for Christmas; the celebration of Christ's birth and His second coming. The question comes at all of us, "Are we ready? Do we have things in order? Are we ready to meet the Lord?" It throws us off a bit as we assume this is a time of levity and celebration. It is, but it's also more: it's a time of preparation. If we are honest with ourselves, we often get caught up in our everyday lives and get busy doing the normal day-to-day things we need to do. We forget to examine what are and where are our priorities. We rarely ask the question about the priorities or even more rarely ask the question, "Are we happy?" Let's face it; we only examine things when we feel we will lose them. So, what's the motivation to examine our lives?

Let's talk about it for a minute. There are lots of people who say why bother living a good or moral life when at the end of our lives, we can just turn to the Lord and say, "Oh yeah, sorry! Whoops! Please forgive me for all my selfishness." According to these people, we are better off living it up and enjoying ourselves in whatever way we want. God must forgive us because He's all-forgiving and all-loving. But what happens if we die before we get a chance to say those words! The reality is that we don't know the time or the hour of our death. So, are we really ready to meet our maker? Instead of playing a game with the Lord we are called to be prepared to meet the Lord at any time. We are called to lead the life of a faithful Christian here and now. That's what the scriptures are telling us today.

Paul's letter to the Romans challenges us to step out of the darkness and into the light, the light of Christ and the truth He bears with His life. Christ is the light of the world and we are called to move toward it. We are called to move out of the darkness of our sins and into the grace of God's presence. We need to ask ourselves how we can move toward the light of truth and be prepared to meet the Lord. Is there anyone with whom I have said words that I need to take back or at the very least be reconciled with? Is there anyone with whom I need to say some words that I need to? Is there some action I must do to be reconciled with my God and our world? Maybe we need to find a way to be kinder and gentler with our children. Maybe we need to find a way to be less demanding of our parents. Maybe we need to find a way to be reconciled with someone in our family or someone in our community that we are at odds with.

Whatever it is, we all have some darkness in our lives in which we need to shine the light of Christ. We are called to wake ourselves up and ask ourselves if we are ready; ready to look at our lives and our priorities and make some changes in preparation for Christmas. We are called to wake ourselves up and not be just swept along with the world's set of priorities, slavishly doing one thing after the next thing. As we come closer to Christmas, this practice of failing to set priorities seems to slip into a higher gear, moving us ever faster along.

The challenge for us then as we begin Advent and our preparation for Christmas is to pause and ask the tough question. Am I ready to meet the Lord? And even more fundamental, we ought to ask that question by a 3-year-old, "Are you happy?"

Being a Good Influence by Being Present!

When I was a child back in Ireland, I had different groups of friends. There were days I would hang out with one group or the other and I always remember what my parents would say after hanging out with one group.

"Brendan, those young boys are not a good influence on you. You have been a brat ever since you started hanging around with them." Then some months later I would have another friend who was just a great guy and they would say "Now that young man is a good boy; you ought to spend more time with him. Actually, you ought to act a little more like him!" You know he was one of those "always-does-it-right boys." So, I dropped him as a friend!! No, I am only kidding…actually, we are still friends.

Maybe you remember such an experience as a child. Or maybe you remember your own children and how their friends can influence them. The reality is that those who we spend time with influence us for good or bad, for better or worse. More to the point, we influence others for good or bad, for better or worse.

In today's Gospel we hear about John the Baptist in the desert, "Preparing the way for the Lord and making straight path." He is fully aware that he is influencing others and he chooses to influence them for the better. John chose to show the way to Christ the Messiah and preached the coming of the Messiah. Clearly, we know that Christ has come so we do not need to preach about the coming of the Messiah, but we can preach the resurrected Christ in our lives by our actions. In other words, we can choose to be a positive influence on others.

As we prepare for Christmas it is easy to get carried away with all the Christmas preparations such as sending Christmas cards, buying gifts, and maybe attending Christmas parties. It seems that this time of year is always so busy. We seem to be consumed by doing different things and often forget to be present to those we are closest. We may forget how we influence others by our actions and our presence.

Brendan McGuire

As we prepare for Christmas this Advent season maybe we can be a positive influence on others by being present to the people who are closest to us. I mean being really present to those around us; our friends, our parents, our children, our teachers or our co-workers. For example, if our spouse or child needs someone to talk to we are willing to genuinely listen and do not put them off with a comment like, "I'm busy right now!" Or if our parent tells us a joke for a laugh, we laugh at their joke, even if it is not funny! Or if our friend needs to cry, we provide a shoulder to cry on.

This week maybe we can be a better influence on those closest to us and prepare the way for Christ by our actions. Maybe it is to listen to others, maybe it is to laugh with others, or maybe it is to cry with others. Whatever way we choose this week may we prepare for the coming of the Lord in our own lives by being good influences and being present to those closest to us.

Third Sunday of Advent
Isaiah 7:10-14; Psalm 24; Romans 1:1-7; Matthew 1:18-24

Work and Wait like a Farmer

Anyone that knows anything about farming knows that farmers work very hard indeed. And while they do their work, they implicitly have great faith and hope in creation and in God's work. Not only do they have great hope, they also have great expectation as well. They hope and expect that the earth will reward the fruit of their labors and that the Lord will bless them with great abundance.

It is this sense of hope and expectation that we hear in the letter of James today. We hear about how we are called to be like farmers. Let's take a closer look at what the farmer does. The farmer does not sit back and wait aimlessly. The farmer goes out and buys the seed. He then tills the land, plants the seed, irrigates and weeds the land. After all that is done, he waits and expects the fruit. He does his work and waits patiently for the land to produce through the grace of God. We'll never see a farmer getting a sack of seeds, throwing them into the barn, then sitting back and waiting for it to grow. That would be absurd.

In other words, the farmer does his share of the work, and then he patiently waits for this fruit, this precious yield of the soil. While he believes and waits for God's presence, the farmer also does his share of the work. Well, that is what we are called to do as disciples. We are called to do our share of the work; to work in the field and do what we are called to do then wait with great expectation for the Lord's presence in our life. Namely, it is in our own hearts that we plant the seed: then we must be willing to till the soil a little too. We must irrigate it with- if you would-works of kindness, works of charity and to pull out the weeds of unforgiveness, resentment and hatred. We are called to tend to this seed - this word of God. And then we can sit and wait for it to blossom forth in our own life as the Prophet Isaiah speaks of today.

But we also understand that waiting is not always easy. Being patient is not always so easy. For example, for those who have grown children, you have planted that seed in their heart and you wonder - will it ever blossom forth; will they ever return to church; will they ever believe in

5

God again; will they ever be active in faith -something you have held dearly, and helped them to understand.

The best way to wait and tend the word of God is for us to continue to plant the seed in our own heart, to continue to till the soil of our own lives, to continue to pluck out those weeds of resentment, unforgiveness and hatred from our own hearts and to irrigate our heart with acts of justice and charity for others. We are called to live out, in word and deed, the word of God we hear.

So, as we leave here today, we are called to be like the farmer and to both work and wait patiently for God, our Immanuel.

God is Always with Us

When I was a child I remember once walking with my father. We were in the bog on a summer night with stars shimmering enough to dispel most of the darkness but not enough to make it bright. I was happy and joyful to be with my father and had no fear of the dark of night. I don't remember exactly at what point but I remember turning around and Dad was gone. Just gone! Suddenly I became terrified. I could hardly see anything in front of me and every noise scared me even further. Then I heard a voice and slowly his image appeared. He was walking towards me. He had just stopped for a minute. My heart stopped pounding and I began to be at ease again. The night did not change but only my perception of it changed. I was happy as long as I knew someone was with me. In this case, it was my father.

In today's scripture we hear God tell us that He is with us always. Through the prophets He said He would send His Son and He would be called Emmanuel which means God-is-with-us. He would be named Jesus which means "God saves." In Jesus, God said two important things. He fulfilled his promise of being with us and more importantly He became one of us to show us the way. He took on our flesh to show us the way. God is with us in every way, in every aspect of human experience, in every adventure we take, in every sorrow we endure. In Jesus, God has pioneered a new way for us to follow. In Jesus, God is within every person through the abiding indwelling presence of the Holy Spirit.

Sometimes in our lives it is easy to see this presence. When things are going well, and our lives are bright it is easy to see and appreciate God. When we have friends and family who are loving. When we have a well-paying job and we have our health. But when things are not so bright, we may begin to doubt whether God is truly with us. When we are in pain, it is sometimes harder to believe. When we lose a friend of many years, whether through death or moving out of town, it may be hard to feel the presence of God. When we are getting old and frail and we cannot do what we used to be able to do and even the most menial task now takes us all day. Or when we are sick, whether physically or emotionally, it seems difficult to see the presence of God. Or when we lose our job. It is like the dark of night and we wonder: where has God gone? The reality is, like my father on that dark night, He is still there. God is still with us. He is always with us. So how do we see that reality?

I believe we can see God-with-us in our community. Each week we gather at this table and acknowledge the presence of Christ in the Eucharist and each other. We gather to offer praise and thanksgiving to God and to renew ourselves in faith and to see the God-with-us in each other, in each and every one of us present here today. Maybe it is one of us who has lost a friend, family member or grown old or in need of comfort. Or maybe there is somebody we know who needs to be comforted and feel the presence of Christ. These last few days before Christmas we can transform our world by taking the joyful presence of Christ to others. Together we can transform the darkness of our lives and together we can celebrate that God is always with us!

And as we leave here today, we can transform the world by allowing ourselves to be transformed at this table, by taking the joy of knowing that God is **always** with us even when we do not see Him.

Ordinary Miracle

Several years ago, there was a movie called *Charlotte's Web*. It is a children's movie about a spider called Charlotte, and a little pig called Wilbur who was rescued by a little girl named Fern. Wilbur ends up in this farmhouse as Fern's pet pig where Charlotte and all the other animals are living. Wilbur and Charlotte develop a friendship that becomes the centerpiece of the storyline of the movie. Charlotte promises to find a way to save Wilbur from the inevitable smokehouse before winter, namely, someone's Christmas dinner.

In an effort to save Wilbur, Charlotte decides to spin a web and spell out words in her web that describe Wilbur and how special he is. The first word she weaves in her web is "some pig". News of this quickly gets around the countryside and draws attention to the barnyard and in turn brings attention to young Wilbur. Charlotte hopes that if Wilbur can win a medal at the County Fair, he will be saved and not be used for bacon! So, as the story goes along, Charlotte continues to spin different words in her web to describe Wilbur. She spells out words like "radiant," "terrific" and "humble" to describe how special he is and what a wonderful friend he has become to all in the barnyard. Unfortunately, Wilbur does not actually win the first-place medal, but he does receive the Fair Governors medal. What Charlotte points out through her words woven in her web about Wilbur are not extraordinary things but only the most ordinary things. The gift that Wilbur gives, the most primary gift that Wilbur gives is one of friendship. He makes Charlotte his friend in the barnyard and makes all the other animals in the barnyard friends. He even makes a friend of the little rascal rat, called Templeton. Wilbur treats them all with respect.

This relationship of Charlotte and Wilbur can be very helpful for us today as we celebrate this feast day of the birth of Christ. We realize today that Christ, in Jesus becoming human, became the most ordinary human being. He was someone very ordinary, just like you and me. Yet there is also something extraordinary that happened. This extraordinary thing was that not only was He the Son of God but that He introduced us to

9

salvation. So now we know we are saved in and through Him. In Christ becoming human we can become divine in time. Now Christ dwells within each one of us. Now that is extraordinary.

Sometimes we can get carried away with Christmas. It's a very real temptation. All year long too we can get carried away with little things –and we forget that ordinary miracles happen in daily life. We can get swept up in the busyness of Christmas, but we also get caught up in the busyness of everyday life. Miracles happen all the time in our daily life, we just do not see it. What Charlotte did in the movie was to point out the ordinary gifts, the ordinary miracles of life.

Today, we have lots of miracles happening to us. It can be just going outside, looking up into the night and seeing the star-studded sky. We forget how it is just an ordinary miracle. Or it can be when we get up in the morning and see a beautiful big blue sky with the sun shining brightly. We forget it's also an ordinary miracle. Or whenever we look out and see the beautiful flowers –even something as simple as a drop of rain falling off that flower –all of it is an ordinary miracle. Or when you look at your children or spouse as they sleep you see how your relationships are ordinary miracles. Each of these is an ordinary miracle that we believe is the presence of Christ to us every day in the ordinary day-to-day events, –the ordinary miracles of our lives.

The movie ends with a great music track called "Ordinary Miracle." These are some of the words on that track:

It's not that unusual when everything is beautiful
It's just another ordinary miracle today.
The sky knows when it's time to snow
Don't need to teach a seed to grow.

Isn't it remarkable?
Like every time a rain drop falls.
The sun comes up and shines so bright It disappears again at night
It's just another ordinary miracle today.

If we can see Christ in the ordinary events of daily life we can once again bring alive the message of Christmas, the Emmanuel, the God-with-us. If we can celebrate the joy of the ordinary moments of every day and not just wait for Christmas, we can celebrate every day of the year by looking and watching for those ordinary miracles. And if we can do what Charlotte does by spinning our webs by not just our words but by our actions, we point also to the humble Christ, the Emmanuel, the God who is always with us.

Wooden Bowl

There is a story about a husband and wife who were happily married and had a four-year-old son. They had a great family routine. Then one day they had to invite their grandfather to live with them. He was old and very frail. His hands trembled, his eyesight was blurred, his hearing was almost completely gone, and his step faltered.

The family ate together at the table each night. But the elderly grandfather's shaky hands and failing sight made eating difficult for him. Food fell easily off his spoon and onto the clean floor. When he grasped the glass, milk spilled on the tablecloth. He often dropped dishes and broke several plates and glasses. The husband and wife became irritated with the mess and how their family routine was disturbed. "We must do something about Granddad," said the man. "I've had enough of his spilled milk, noisy eating, and food on the floor. I don't know how many more dishes we will go through!"

So, the husband and wife set a small table in the corner. There, Granddad ate alone while the rest of the family enjoyed dinner at the main table. Since the old man had broken several dishes, he was given a wooden bowl and plastic fork. When the family glanced toward grandfather's direction, sometimes he had a tear in his eye as he sat alone. Even so, when he dropped a plastic fork or spilled food from his wooden bowl the only words the couple had for him were sharp. The four-year-old watched it all in silence.

Several weeks later, the man noticed his son playing with wood blocks, trying to carve a hole in the largest block. He asked the child sweetly, "What are you making?" Just as sweetly, the boy responded, "Oh, I am making a little bowl for you and Mama to eat your food in when I grow up." The four-year-old smiled and went back to work. The words so struck the parents that they were speechless. Then tears started to stream down their cheeks. Though no word was spoken, both knew what had to be done. That evening the husband took Granddad's hand and gently led him back to the family table. For the remainder of his days he ate every meal with the family. For some reason, they did not care about how many more dishes were broken, or how much food spilled onto the table or how much food fell to the floor. Granddad was back at the table and that was okay with them.

Today, we celebrate the feast of the Holy Family and in so many ways, each one of our families can be a grace-filled and holy family. But oftentimes we get hard-headed with each other because there are little irritations that rub on us; there are little things that we do to each other that make it hard to be that "happy family." Today's letter to the Colossians speaks about the family and how we are called to honor one another. We are called to be caring and loving for one another and in all things to put on love and in particular to always do everything in Christ for one another.

In today's first reading, Sirach goes even further with his wisdom, namely, how we are called to treat our parents. When they get old and frail, we are called to treat them with kindness and love. I'm not saying it's easy because it's not. When Grandpa does come to join the table, he probably will make a mess and he probably will spill and break dishes. That is the reality of when we get old and frail. We cannot hear like we used to. We certainly cannot see like we used to and we most certainly cannot walk or do things like we used to. But we are called to be kind and gentle and most especially with our elders; they are frail, and they have put in their days of work for us. Now I know they are not perfect. They've got their foibles and they've got their weaknesses and maybe they weren't even the best of parents to us. But they are our parents or grandparents and we must care for them with kindness and humility.

Today as we celebrate the Holy Family, let's look around and look for opportunities in which we can care for one another most especially the elderly, our parents, and our grandparents who have become frail beyond our own imagining. May we be kind and loving and caring in every way.

Feast of the Epiphany
Isaiah 60:1-6; Psalm 138; Ephesians 3:2-3a, 5-6; Matthew 2:1-12

Nine Miles Apart

Jerusalem and Bethlehem are only nine miles apart yet in so many ways they are light years apart. Jerusalem is a sign of power, wealth and opulence; Bethlehem is a much smaller town, just nine miles away; it is more of a "stop-over town" where people would only stay on their journey to somewhere else. There is little power and wealth there, even to this day.

The Magi in today's Gospel expected to see the newborn king to come from the great city of Jerusalem. So, the Magi sought the wisdom of King Herod to find his whereabouts. But King Herod turns to his theologians and inquires of them as to where this king is to be born. They inform him the newborn king will come from Bethlehem, a small town nine miles away.

There are two very important things that come out of this Gospel, the Lord does not always operate in ways we think, and the reaction of the scribes. God does not come to the great City of Jerusalem but instead to a humble town, Bethlehem. For us in our lives, it is not in the great and glorious moments of our day that God seems to be clearly known to us. In fact, it is probably in the humbler parts of our day that we more clearly see our God at work. It is often not in the great days of our lives when everything is going very well that we see our God. Rather, it is more often when things are not going well; in the darker parts of our lives, that we seek that star, that little light shine, and we are drawn back to the Christ in our lives.

It seems to me that when things are going well for us, when we have our friends and our family, when we have a good job and everything seems to be going well, that is when we seem to get caught up in the world of Jerusalem, so to speak. We easily get caught up in the good happenings of our world and forget about our God and his presence in our lives. We give the same attention to God like that of the Scribes: we say, "Yeah. Yeah. I know He is here or there." But we don't change our ways in any way. Like the Scribes who say, "The king won't be born here; He will be born in Bethlehem." But the Scribes and theologians did not go with the

Magi; they stayed behind and experienced no conversion. Instead the Magi followed that bright but tiny star and they experienced the Christ; they had a change of heart and mind. We are called to have that change of mind and heart, to allow Christ to shine His light in our lives, and to recognize and to see that light wherever we are in our lives.

Most often it seems to be only in the dark times of our lives that we are even ready to hear or see where God is operating. We look readily for God in those dark moments and struggle when we do not see Him. Yet, isn't it true we believe God is present to us in all times? It is my conviction that we don't have to wait until things are not going well. We don't have to wait until we have bad health to be grateful for having good health. We don't have to wait until we lose our job to be grateful for having a job. We don't have to wait until we lose our family, or until we have a big fight in our family, to be grateful for the gift of our family.

My hope as we begin a New Year is that we truly live the epiphany in our own lives, and to look not just into the dark part of our lives but also in the times that are going well. To look at your spouse and your children and to celebrate the gift of them in your life. To be able to look at the people you work with and the people who are alongside of you and to celebrate having a job. To look at what we have here in San Jose and be grateful for all that God has blessed us with. To see and look at where God's hands are in the midst of our lives. Yes, we believe God is present at all times, but we are often distracted by the "Jerusalem's" of our lives, the good times of our lives.

As we start a new year, we are called to open our eyes once anew and to allow God to make Himself known, to manifest Himself. We need to take the time to notice the good things we have in our life and to celebrate those good things and to not wait for the darkness to come. But it is not enough to settle ourselves in the bright light of things going well for us, but to reach out to others who might be experiencing the dark times in their lives. It is our opportunity to be the light of the world to them; to be that light of Christ for others to see.

If we are experiencing that darkness in our lives right now, we need to know that a star does shine in the midst of our darkness and that God will guide us through it. We need to know and believe that God is with us, even in that darkest period of our life and that we can choose to believe it.

Today, we celebrate the Epiphany, the Christ, the light of our world. We have come to recognize Him not just in the dark times of our life but also in the good times in our life. We recognize that Christ is the light of the world and we come to share that good news with others.

Words of Affirmation

Any good coach or good manager will know that to get the best out of people, we sometimes have to challenge them to go beyond their limitations of what they think they can do. Good coaches do this, and great managers do it. But good coaches also know there is great importance in balancing that challenge with words of affirmation; to have some words of encouragement when they do well. For example, a coach will say to somebody when they have done a great play in sports, "Hey great job; great play; great teamwork." Or a manager will say to a staff member in the midst of some long project, "Hey, great job, well done, thank you for hanging in there and making that happen on time." All those are important realities of balancing a challenge with words of affirmation.

That is why it is so encouraging for us to hear the Gospel today, to hear the words of affirmation come from God to Christ His son. Christ, who was about to begin His public ministry is given the words of affirmation by God Himself through His spirit, "Here is my beloved Son in whom I am well pleased." It is encouraging for us because if Christ needs it, then it is logical to conclude that you and I need it too. So, when was the last time that we have encouraged those around us in the practice of their faith? We are great at encouraging people in sports and academics. It is popular these days to give an award for just about everything. There is even such a thing as "a participation award." It is given to all who just show up! Maybe we need to start doing that for our practice of faith!

We could all do with a little affirmation in the ways of faith. For example, those of you who are here today, when was the last time you congratulated your child on coming to church with you? Or when was the last time that you congratulated them or commended them for doing some good kind act for their siblings or for somebody else? For the children who are present here today, when was the last time you said to Mom and Dad, "Thank you for taking me to church"? It works both ways.

We must encourage each other in our faith. Every single one of us can find something else to do on a Sunday morning. We don't have to be here.

17

We chose to be here and sometimes it is important to encourage each other. Father Edgar or I can get up here and say thank you for being at church but so many of you just let that roll off you because most of you think, "Well what do you expect, that's Father; he is going to say what he is paid to say." But seriously, it is so good to see so many of you here today and it is important to affirm each other in doing that.

I understand there are many other things that we could be doing instead of coming to church; like sleeping in for instance. But today you chose to be here and to be one with us in the faith. It is so important to not just come to church on Sunday but to also do the ordinary things that we do for each other on a daily basis, like encouraging discussions about faith. Whenever your children come home from school and are struggling with something that happened that day, it is important to be able to talk to them about it in the context of faith and encourage them when they are making decisions based in faith. There are other times when they do an act of kindness for somebody and we know they don't have to. Yes, we need to point that out and thank them for acting like a Christian, affirming one another in our faith together. We all need it.

It is not that I don't want you to continue to challenge each other. We all need to continue to challenge, just like any sports coach or good manager, a good parent also knows they need to challenge each other, to push each other to do just a little bit more. We also need to balance it out with words of affirmation.

So whether we are a child being encouraged by our parents or whether we are a child encouraging our parents for the acts of kindness they do, or whether it is amongst friends, today as we renew ourselves not just in our own Baptism, but in His Baptism we see Christ taking on the sins of the world. He comes now and His public ministry is confirmed by God Himself saying this is His beloved Son in whom He is well pleased. May we also say it to one another that we are well pleased with one another and that we encourage each other in faith.

Destined for Great Work

At age 70, Michelangelo wrote to his nephew Leonardo; "Many believe–as I believe–that I was designated by God to do the work that I do. Even now in my old age, I cannot stop doing this work because I love what I do, and I am called by God to do it."

Michelangelo was one of the greatest artists that ever walked this planet. He was also an incredibly humble man who gave all the credit to God. He recognized that everything he did was in and through Christ and God worked wonders through him. In his later years, he was famed for his humility. For example, when he was carving or sculpting a new piece of work, he protested when somebody would say, "How do you carve and etch that out of that blank rock?" He would retort, "It is not I who carves something new. All I do is set free what the Lord has inside the rock." He had the profound humility of understanding that his role in his art was that of only being an instrument of God.

Today we hear in three different readings a similar message; all the characters in the readings are pointing to God and to Christ. In the first reading, the Prophet Isaiah is pointing to the new Messiah, the suffering servant, who we believe is Christ Jesus. He says that this suffering servant will change everything for the people; He will be a light to all the world. In the second reading, Paul starts his greeting to the Corinthians by telling them that it is in and through Christ that we are all saved. In the Gospel of John, we hear how John the Baptist warns that it is not about what he does but instead it is about the Lamb of God. Christ is He, the one who takes away the sin of the world. It is Christ that John points to and it is because of Christ that John must decrease and Christ must increase. It is in that sense of profound humility that we are called to act as disciples. It is that ability to not take credit for something ourselves, but to say it is God who works in me.

Michelangelo was not always so humble. In his younger years, a tourist came to Rome and gave credit to Michelangelo's contemporary, Cristoforo Solari, for one of the Pieta that he had seen. Michelangelo became so enraged when he heard of it that he took a hammer and chisel, went to

19

the piece of work and chiseled his name in it, "Michelangelo Buonarroti made this." From the very moment he etched his name in there, he regretted having done so. From that moment on he never signed a single piece of work for he knew, in that moment of weakness, he betrayed the gift that God had given him. From then on, he knew that all he had done was God working through Christ in him and truly believed that until his dying day. You and I are called to do that same thing: to work our hardest to unveil and to develop the gift that God has given us; to develop that gift God has designed us to be and to let that come free so that we become the work of art He wants us to be. We are called to work hard at making that happen in our own life. When we do accomplish great things, we are called to not take the credit for ourselves but instead point the message back to what God does in us and through us. To point back to what Christ enables us to do through His strength and through His direction by the Holy Spirit.

It is that sense of humility that we are called to search for and to harness. Yet, it is so tempting when we do a good job on something to sign our name: "Brendan McGuire did this!" The temptation is very real, to just scrawl our name on it and take credit for it. Somebody will say something like, "Oh yeah, that was my idea. Yup. All my idea." Sometimes we even make projects out of our own children. We take our child as if this is a masterpiece we are creating and take the credit for their every grade. We say things like, "Oh yeah, my son has all first-rate honors." "*My son*" as if it were "my grades" and "my credits." It is great for us to enable them to do all the good things they do. But it is not our work. It is God working in and through us and in and through them that they do it. We are called to be able to stand back just a little and say, "Not I but the Christ within me who does the work."

No matter what we are trying to accomplish, whether it's great things in sports, academics or just in the ordinary achievements of daily life at work or at home, it is much easier to say it than to do it. We want to do the best we can, and we want to show others that we have done the best we can. We want to make sure that we point it back to God's Spirit within us.

I know that sounds easy, but it is not so easy to do. The only way I know how to do this is to bring into our own prayer life that sense of reflection of what it is that I am doing and for whom I am doing it. We must realize that often the greatest ideas we get just pop into our head and we think, "Where did that come from?" We know that it did not come from us; it came out of nowhere but nobody else knows that and are we tempted to say, "Yeah, yeah. It was my idea." Instead we need to let go of that ownership and realize that we are just instruments of God. We are very important instruments, each and every one of us, like Michelangelo, destined for great work. Although we may not paint the Sistine Chapel or sculpt some of the greatest art in history, we have a role to play. Our role is to point the way to Christ in all we say and all we do and to take no credit but to give it to Christ.

Taking Down the Christmas Light,
Not the Light of Christ

With a break in the weather from the recent rain, I had the opportunity to do something that I have been reluctant to do for the past several weeks. I took down the Christmas lights from outside my house. It is always with great reluctance that I do so because when I take down the Christmas lights, I always feel that I am putting away the spirit of Christmas. As I took down the lights, what the neighbors did not realize was that the inside of the house was still fully lit up with the Christmas tree and all my decorations were still there. Slowly, I concluded that I must take those down too and reluctantly disassembled everything and put them all away. The house looked so plain; so boring and so dull again. However, I had a little plug-in night-light with a little Christmas tree, so I kept that one to keep Christmas in the house.

Sometimes we are tempted into thinking that when we take down our Christmas lights and put them all away, we might put away the spirit of Christmas. We must not give in to that temptation. The lights of Christmas are not just decorations of the holiday season brightening up our homes. They are a reminder for us of the light of Christ; the light that stays within our own hearts. We are called to keep that light of Christ burning brightly all year round; to never let it be extinguished, to never let it get down to just a sparkle. Instead we ought to keep it burning brightly amid the darkness of the winter of our lives.

I have always loved Christmas because it comes in the middle of the darkness. We turn on these bright lights and it seems to send joy into our hearts. It seems so appropriate then to keep the light of Christ burning too. We are called to carry that same joy with us throughout the year, not just in the Christmas season.

Today, in the first reading, the Prophet Isaiah predicts the light that would shine in the darkness of the people's lives. Christians, as the Gospel clarifies today, have seen a fulfillment of that prophesy in Jesus Christ, the light of the world coming into humanity to shine a light into the darkness of all humanity. That light continues to burn brightly for us

22

now, some 2000 years later. We now become that light of Christ to others. And therefore, for us, who are called Christians, we must make sure that the spirit of Christmas, the light of Christmas, the light of Christ is kept burning brightly within our hearts. The way we do that is through simple things. Never underestimate the power of a simple smile to somebody who has had a bad day. Never underestimate the power of a kind and gentle comment to somebody who is experiencing a rough patch in their life. Or in these darker days, when people find it hard to go outside in the rain, to never underestimate the power of a visit to an elderly or sick neighbor, who has not been out for days or even weeks. What simple joy that visit can bring. The light that a visit brings to their darkness is immense. Those are the little things that we are called to be for others. We are called to be that light through our words and our actions, and to keep that flame bright and burning.

Today, the second reading from Paul to the Corinthians reminds us that every action is always meant to be about Christ. We must always focus our attention on Christ in this world and always remember that you and I are called to be that Christ to others. Through our little actions of gentleness, kindness, patience and yes, even forgiveness for those who have hurt us, we can turn on the light and dispel the darkness of doubt, of pain and sometimes even suffering.

But I think there is one more thing we need to learn. It is very important that we hold on to it, especially during these darker days after Christmas. It is the joy of Christmas. We must learn to laugh and learn to see the humor of life and not allow ourselves to be burdened or taken down by life's troubles. This is not to negate or pretend that these problems aren't there, but to put them all in perspective against the cosmic realities of our lives. Think about all the things we get preoccupied with on a daily basis; the stuff with the kids doing their homework, the endless tasks we have to do as parents, the effort of taking care of elderly parents, the things that people have said or done to us over the years, what we have said or done to them. We find that in the greater scope and context of our lives and in that greater context and scope of all eternity, they are all very small. Yet, we get so preoccupied with them.

Instead, I think we are called to grasp a hold of this light and to let it shine, to let it burn brightly and to see the joy that life can give us. To see the gift of being able to get up even if it is raining outside; the gift, even if it is raining, to be able to go out for a walk. The gift of health gives us the benefit of being able to have a new day, a new dawn each and every day. Now, that is joy, a new day. But we must choose to live that joy, and when we do so, we give others light in the midst of their darkness.

So as we leave here nourished from the table, nourished from seeing one another gather at this table, and as we pack away our Christmas lights, may we not pack away the light of Christ, but instead may we choose by our every action of gentleness, loving, kindness, patience, forgiveness, and most of all by the joy in which we live our lives, to keep the light of Christ burning brightly in our hearts.

Make Room for Christ

Two teenage boys accompanied their father to the Christmas Eve celebration of the Mass at their parish. When they reached the church, there was a huge crowd of people outside. They could not even get near the door. Frustrated, the two teenage boys looked over at their father and said, "Oh, c'mon Dad. This is ridiculous. Wouldn't we be better off going downtown and just serve the homeless instead of standing here, watching other people pray?"

It is an interesting question if you think about it. How would you genuinely answer it? I know that the first instinct would be to say both. And yes, it is both, coming to church and reaching out to others in need. But what if you were given a choice? What if your teenage son or daughter asked you that question: To serve the homeless and the needy or go to church? What would your answer be? I know we would like to say both, but, if we had to choose, I suspect we would end up saying serving the needy. Not that we would ever want to make that choice but living out the Word is the single most important thing we could do.

That is the exact issue the Prophet Zephaniah tries to address today. He is trying to inspire these people, who are no longer living the word, but still giving words of worship. They no longer have any fire in their belly, so he tries to inspire them and says, "Look, I am going to take a remnant from you, some small part of you, will come and follow the word of God, and then others in future generations will know that there is a God of mercy. There is only one God, the Lord of Hosts."

It is a similar issue that Paul addresses in his letter to the Corinthians. The people get carried away with the oratory skills of Apollos and lose sight of the message. Instead, Paul tells them, "Look, the message is always about Christ." It does not make any difference where you came from, or what you used to do. We are all called to live out the word of God in our life. It is always about Christ, not about those wonderful words we might hear. It is about the Word and how we live our daily life.

25

In today's scripture reading from the Gospel of Matthew, we hear the beginning of the great Sermon on the Mount, the Beatitudes. It is here that Jesus lays out very clear mandates about what we are called to do. We are blessed if we do all the things that He asks us to do. These are hard words to hear. How is poverty a good thing, or sorrow a good thing? In and of themselves, these do not seem to be good things and I do not think they are, but when we are in those places, it is what happens to us that bring about the blessedness.

You must understand that this was a real reversal of roles. In Jesus' time, anyone who was healthy, or wealthy was considered to be blessed by God. Those who were poor, unhealthy or sick in any way were considered in some way to be cursed by God. That was the understanding at the time. Then along comes Jesus, and He says, no. He turns it upside down. He turns it around and says blessed are the poor; blessed are the sorrowful; blessed are those who are meek and humble. The difference is that when we are in a place of poverty in spirit or in actual poverty, then we have room for God. When we are sick, we tend to turn to God. When we are humble, we make room for God in our hearts. That is the challenge. These things create in us a space for God to be. When all our needs are met, when we are healthy, we often forget about our God. And that is why there is a real reversal here.

Dietrich Bonhoeffer, a great German theologian, priest and pastor, was executed by the Nazis for his Christian beliefs. He wrote that the main turning point in his discipleship was his reflection on this very passage. He found it difficult and struggled over this passage from the beginning of the Sermon on the Mount. Could it be possible that our God has asked us to live these radical beatitudes in our life, or are these just some high-flying goals that really no one can attain? Out of his reflections on this very passage, Bonhoeffer concluded that the Lord really is calling us to live this poverty, to live this version of discipleship. He maintains this because Christ Himself lived it.

Christ was the one who was poor in spirit; Christ was the one who was humble; Christ was the one who was a peacemaker. Christ was the one who lived every one of those beatitudes and therefore we are called to walk in the footsteps of Jesus. If we are to be followers of Christ, then we are called to follow in His footsteps of being humble and poor in spirit. - As Dietrich Bonhoeffer says, to make room in our heart for

God, to be poor in spirit, not because we want poverty, but because we want to make room in our heart for God. So, for those who are poor, we have empathy to make room in our hearts for sorrow. For those who are in pain and in sorrow, we have empathy to make room in our hearts for meekness and humility. For those who are humble and meek, we have empathy with, and grow to be like them.

Today, we do not need to make a choice between praying or acting out our faith; instead we must now do what we pray here. We must go out of here making sure we walk in the footsteps of Christ, to ensure that we act like Christ to others, to be poor in spirit, to be humble, to be sorrowful so that we can identify with those who are in those places and to leave room in our heart for God. Today, we choose not only to worship in word, but we also choose to walk in the footsteps of Christ and make room for God in our hearts.

We <u>Are</u> Salt of the Earth!

A wedding guest was asked to give a toast at a friend's wedding. At the reception, as the glasses were raised, the guest presented the couple with a beautifully wrapped gift. Inside the box was salt—ordinary table salt. At first the couple was perplexed. Then he offered the toast. "It's hard to keep a house without salt. It adds flavor and taste to just about every dish. And if you run out of toothpaste, you can brush with a mixture of soda and salt because of salt's cleansing qualities. And if you develop a sore throat, you can gargle with salt because of its healing qualities. And if you are hungry you can cure a ham or other meat because of its preserving qualities. You can also use salt to melt ice that builds up in the winter cold or you can use salt to put out fires that flare up." He closed his toast by saying, "So if you bring to your marriage the qualities found in salt —the cleansing quality, the healing quality, the preserving quality; if you use it to enhance the flavor of your lives together; to melt the ice that will occasionally build up and put out the flames that will occasionally flare up between you; and of course, if you take everything with a grain of it, you will have a long happy marriage."

Yes indeed, if we all could live according to that toast! In today's Gospel Jesus tells His disciples, and us, that they, and we, are the light of the world and salt of the earth. Not that we will <u>become</u> the light of the world or <u>become</u> salt of the earth. But that we <u>are.</u>

In choosing to follow Jesus Christ we are the light of the world and the salt of the earth. We are because Christ works in and through us. We are because it is Christ who makes us shine or taste with flavor. Jesus draws a direct connection between who we are and what we do. He says that all disciples are called to live for <u>others</u>. We do not hide our salvation, our grace, or our new life. Instead we show what a difference it makes in our life. We are called to show how Christ makes a difference in our life. We are called to be light to the world and salt of the earth.

Notice that qualities of salt referred to in the wedding guest's toast are all qualities that add to something or someone else. When added to food it gives flavor, when added to soda it cleans, when added to wounds it heals, when added to meats it preserves, when added to ice it melts and when added to fire it extinguishes. All its qualities depend upon it being shared.

We too are called as disciples to share who we are. We are called to bring our salt to others. We are called to be the salt of joy and laughter that brings goodness to those around us. We are called to be the salt of forgiveness that heals our families and friends of estrangement and pain. We are called to be the salt of love that binds our relationships with lasting fidelity.

As we continue on our journey of faith together, challenged and called to be salt of the earth may we be mindful that it is only in the sharing of our very selves with others that we are truly the salt of the earth.

Thermometer or Thermostat

Today's Gospel is a continuation of the Sermon on the Mount that we started two weeks ago with the Beatitudes. Last week we continued with the sermon of the salt and the light analogy which further illustrates what we are called to be today. In today's passage, Christ takes it one step further telling His disciples that He has not come to abolish the law but that He has come to fulfill the law. Indeed, He goes even further and says that not even one part of the law will be taken away, not even one stroke will be taken away, but we need to live even more than the law. Today, He gives three illustrations of that demand which seem almost incomprehensible: not only must we do what is required in the law, as the Scribes and Pharisees, but we need to go even further. He says we must not only not kill someone but we must not even be angry with them; that we must not only not commit adultery against someone but we must not even lust after somebody; that we must not only not swear falsely but we must not swear at all.

It is not only just about the letter of the law but the spirit of the law. In other words, it is not enough just to check off like some to-do list our observance of the law, but we must live the spirit of the law as well. Oftentimes we have done something right, but we have failed to live the spirit of the law as it speaks of a much deeper reality in our hearts. So how are we to understand this? Think of it in terms of different purposes: think of the difference between a thermometer and a thermostat! A thermometer just tells you what the temperature is; it is a static reality; it reflects only what the environment is; it tells you if it is hot, if it is cold, or if it is lukewarm. A thermostat on the other hand sets the temperature of the room. It's the instrument that takes in what the temperature of the room is and then moves the temperature of the room in the direction in which you desire it to go. In other words, it is the instrument that sets the temperature of the room.

That is the way of our discipleship. We know, as Christians, we are called to do more than what other people do because that is only acting like a thermometer. We just reflect to what other people do. "Well, I am only doing what other people do. Why do other people get away with that? Why can't I get away with that? Nobody else is reaching out to the poor!" We are merely doing what other people are doing.

Last weeks' Gospel is an illustration of how we are called to be more than people just reflecting what society is; we are called to be salt for the earth and light for the world. We are called to set the temperature of society by our actions; by who we are; to set the bar at a new level. That is what Christ means when He says to be a person, not just of the letter of the law but to live by the spirit of the law.

So how does that work in our own lives? It requires that not only do we forgive when somebody forgives us but that we are the first one to forgive. We set the temperature. We don't wait to respond to the temperature of the society around us. That we are the ones who reach out —not because other people are doing it but because we set the temperature and we decide this is what we are; this is who we are; this is what we will do because we are Catholic Christians. We are part of the Holy Spirit community and that is what we do. We don't wait to respond. We set the temperature. We are thermostats.

So, the question then is how does that work in our own lives? It works in each one of us in slightly different ways. If we are in school, then setting the temperature means that we are going to be the one to go back and try to make peace in the group of friendships. We are going to be the one who is going to be the first to forgive and to try to make things work for our friends. At the office, that might be the same scenario. Certainly, in the home, we are called to set a higher bar, a higher temperature that we know the Lord has chosen us to be. We are called to be the salt of the earth and the light of the world. That does not come without us putting in some effort. It will not happen just by us merely responding to whatever everyone else is doing. Anyone can do that. Instead, we are called to be Catholic Christians who make a difference.

Today, we come to celebrate at the table; to receive strength for what that work is because that is some serious work to do. We are not thermometers of society reflecting what society gives us; we set a new temperature because we are thermostats of Christ Jesus.

Ambassadors for Christ

Over the last few months, there was a great scandal that broke in the world through something called "Wiki-leaks." The scandal was about the release of private documents shared between diplomats around the world, mostly U.S. diplomats. The release of those documents, and making them public, caused great embarrassment for the diplomats because their private thoughts and words were captured and made public.

What I find interesting is that people understand our diplomats or ambassadors needed to have a certain amount of latitude to do what they needed to do as diplomats. In fact, there was a massive backlash against Wiki-leaks and the founders of Wiki-leaks themselves because people believe our diplomats need some room to do their work. Yes, we want our diplomats to hold up to a high standard, but they also need to have room to do what they need to do which is to put our nation on the best foot forward.

I was part of a discussion group talking about the ethics behind such practices. It was interesting because we wound up talking about the value and the meaning of an ambassador or a diplomat of a country. The importance is that they speak for the country and they represent the country in good and powerful ways. We realize they have human limitations, but we do not expect them to misbehave in any way; we have a high standard for their behavior and so there is a low tolerance for failure and a high expectation for good morals.

Today, in Paul's letter to the Corinthians, he is admonishing the Corinthians to be ambassadors for Christ. He is very aware that the Corinthian community is a divided community; they have been broken by scandal if you would. He is now asking them to step up and raise the bar; to be men and women who are diplomats in the Lord's name. That would mean they would have a higher standard to their behavior, and he asks them to be ambassadors for Christ.

The Church chooses this reading for today, Ash Wednesday and it is the same reading every Ash Wednesday. It is a reminder that our journey in Lent is a recalling for every single one of us as disciples that we are called to be a diplomatic attaché if you would for Christ. It is up to you and me to be that official representative to the world. The understanding is that the world needs official representatives. The world needs people to have their best foot put forward so the world can look at you and me and see there's a Christian; there is somebody who follows Christ. That is what it means to be a Christian.

Now if we are honest and we just reflect on this last week, maybe even the last 24 hours and we put in public every comment and every word that we have said, would we have a Wiki-leak scandal? It might not make the headlines, but we know for the most part that you and I would be at the very least embarrassed because not every action, not every word and most certainly not every thought is something we would want to have published.

You see the journey of Lent is a reminder for us to keep our focus on Christ. It is a reminder for us to purify ourselves, to focus and cut away what we do not need; to focus on Christ Jesus simple and pure. The journey of Lent gives us the three-fold way, three things to do to help us with that process and they are very effective if we do them. Number one is to pray. If we focus our hearts in prayer, if we come back to the moment in prayer and listen to what God has to say to our innermost heart then we will hear what we need to let go of and what we need to not say. So, the first thing we need to commit to, in the next 40 days, is a little more prayer.

The next two things are not only closely tied together, they are tied together in a very important way. One of them is fasting and the other is alms giving. Traditionally, for Lent we have given up something. But Lent isn't just about giving up something for the sake of giving up something. We give up something so that we can give something away. It is about repentance and the sacrifice of giving up something and so therefore we give alms. We fast from something so that we can give something away, they go hand in hand. For example, if we were to give up candy, we would save whatever money we would have spent on candy and give it to the poor. It doesn't mean that we give up candy for all of Lent and store it up and then pig-out on Easter Sunday, which is what I think I did when I was a kid. But that is the problem; we have lost the art of fasting. Without a purpose, our fasting becomes meaningless. So, we have prayer at the top, fasting so that we can give alms and we do all of this as an internal reality.

On Ash Wednesday we distribute ashes. Sometimes I find it is such a total contradiction to the Gospel —what we do in secret says the Gospel, we now put on our forehead and we do publicly. It is a struggle, right? This refers to the journey of Lent. This refers to us being marked with Christ. This refers to I am owned by Christ. I am Christ's. It is a reminder that I am an ambassador of Christ. And so, we wear that as a badge, maybe not of honor, but a badge that says everything I do today is for Christ. That means we must be very careful of what we say and what we do and maybe even what we think.

If not for any other day on our Lenten journey, if for today while we wear the ashes on our forehead, let us be ambassadors for Christ. For today, if not on any other day, let us practice our prayer today; let us practice our giving up so we can give away and remember we are Christ's and it is Christ who we represent with that ash. We are ambassadors for Christ.

Listening to the Right Sounds

There is an ancient Greek myth that speaks of how the sirens used to play such beautiful sweet music on the Greek Islands that any of the ships passing by would be lured in by the music. The sailors would come closer and closer to the island to see where the music was coming from. As they got closer, they would get sucked all the way into the harbor where the Greeks would attack them and take all the merchandise from their ship.

The music was so sweet and so melodious that no sailor could pass anywhere close to the Greek Islands without being lured into this trap by the music of the sirens. So much so that when sailors passed the Greek Islands, they would put wax into their ears and refuse to hear the lure of the music. Even then, the beautiful sound could be heard through the wax and the sailors would pursue the music to see where it was coming from.

Orpheus was a wise man and the captain of several vessels. When he passed the Greek Islands, he took out his lyre and played a more magnificent melody which was even more harmonious and sweet than the music the Greeks could produce so his sailors only listened to his music and were never lured into the islands, ever.

In our own time, I think we all get lured by the sound of the voices and music of our world that lures us away from what we know is often the right choice. The music from the world is often so sweet that we find ourselves being drawn in and destroyed by the very thing that we hear. For example, the lure and voices of our world tell us that we need to buy the latest gadget for everything. We haven't even used the other one yet! The latest iPhone; or the latest Droid; the latest computer! It doesn't stop with the computers and gadgets; it is clothes too. "Oh, that's out of fashion. We need to buy some clothes." Then we must have a new pair of shoes! There is nothing wrong with the old shoes, but the voices tell us they are no longer fashionable. We've got to get this; we've got to get that. We need a bigger house; we want a bigger car and the list goes on and on. And the music sounds so sweet. Even though it sounds so good, we know inside our hearts that we can get trapped and destroy ourselves in the midst.

It is not just outside voices that tempt and lure us; it is also sometimes the inner voice: the inner voice of self-doubt or maybe the inner voice of grudges or hatreds that we hold onto. Yes, indeed, their music sounds so compelling that we are lured into moving closer to them. In the end we know that it is destroying us; we know that somehow these voices are luring us away from what the Lord asks us to do.

Today's Gospel and first reading show us what to do with these alternative voices. In the first reading, we hear the epic story of the fall of Adam and Eve: that Eve listened to the serpent, as an alternative voice from God, followed that voice into the harbors of danger and found herself destroyed and Adam with her. They both got sucked into the sweet sound of Satan's voice which we now call sin. Anything that causes us to turn away from God is what we call sin.

In today's Gospel, Jesus spends 40 days in the desert and here He is tempted again and again - tempted to listen to a voice other than God's. In this case, Jesus was tempted to use His divine power to change stone into bread instead of being human and recognizing His own limitations as human. Most of all, He only wanted to do His Father's will.

We will not be tempted in that same way. I don't think that any of us will be going to the desert any time soon to starve for 40 days. We are probably not going to be listening to any serpents to be tempted to eat out of a tree either. But we will get tempted by voices other than the Lord's. We can be like those sailors and stick wax in our ears, but we know that the voices, the music of temptation will continue to play in the world.

The music of the commercial world will continue to play, and the voices of temptation will continue to speak —that we can be assured of. But we need to attune our minds to the voice and music of God so that we are not so easily lured away. Instead, we remain focused on His voice and what He wants us to do. That sounds great but how do we do that?

The three-fold focus for our journey of Lent is prayer, fasting and almsgiving. The first and most important is prayer. I don't know any other way in which to focus our attention on God's will unless it is through prayer. It is in prayer that we come to recognize God's voice and know the melodious tune of the Lord whom we claim to follow. It takes practice. It requires us to take some time on our Lenten journey to sit and listen to the Lord's voice. In those quiet moments we can replay the things that happened in our day asking ourselves if we could have handled situations better; if we could have been a little bit kinder; if we could have been a little less judgmental; if we could have been more forgiving; if we could have done something to help a situation go slightly better.

Every one of us here is going to be dealing with something slightly different; we are all unique individuals and we all have different challenges. But for sure, every single one of us will have temptation; we will have temptations to listen to voices other than the Lord. The challenge for us is to come to know that voice and to truly listen to that voice; to not be distracted by temptation but to focus on Christ Himself.

This week as we start our Lenten journey with renewed conversion, let us really want to renew the commitment to that conversion; let us commit to more prayer, to listening to Christ, to listen to that voice and to heed the music of His voice.

Before and After

I am sure you have seen the advertisements on television and in newspapers
with the pictures of people "before" and "after." Some of those
advertisements are for dental whitening. The before picture shows
someone with the look of a sad face; then after whitening, bling! White
teeth and all bright smiles. Other advertisements are for diets. On the
before picture you see some slumped figures; the after picture shows
a nice slim person barely recognizable as the same person. And some
advertisements are for exercise machines. On the before picture you
see a rather plumpish person; then afterwards they have a perfectly
sculptured body.

With the "before picture" the marketers are trying to identify with us. That
is sad. Right? They are trying to identify with us or get us to identify
with the picture. The "after picture" is meant to inspire us. They try to
somehow lure us into buying their product or their program that will
help with this transformation from before to after. What they do not tell
you about is the stuff in between. And that is the part of the magic—
that you do not see that.

In today's Gospel, we hear of a similar transformation called the
transfiguration. We have Jesus, who identifies completely and wholly
to us as humans. The Son of God literally becomes one of us, a human,
in Jesus. And now on the top of this mountain, the disciples see Him
transfigured before their eyes. It is now clear that Jesus is really the divine
Son of God. In Matthew's Gospel, we are always called as His disciples
to be what Christ is. We are always called to walk where Christ walked
and to do as Christ did. And so for us, we are to be transfigured as well;
our lives are meant to be transformed and our lives are meant to go
through this constant transformation in discipleship. This started for us
as Christians at our baptism where we were transformed and were made
new. We became different people. Unlike the mysterious change that
took place all in one flash like Christ, our transformation happens over a
lifetime. We need to understand that the "before" and "after" pictures of
our lives require us to commit to a lot of transformation during our lives.

For example, for the people who go on diets, there is a whole lot of not eating that goes on! No matter what diet program one takes, there is a whole lot of not eating! There is no way of getting around that fact. No matter how magical the process may seem, there is a lot of hard work in dieting. The same goes for those wonderful workout machines. No matter what way you cut it, there is a whole lot of working out that one must do. There is a whole lot of hard sweat and probably some dieting that also goes on. The change is not so magical after all. The results are sharp and distinct between the before and after but the in between is where the work is.

So too it is with our spiritual lives as Christians. It is not so much a magical transformation as it is the hard work of every day choosing to do what God would have us do. Every day, slugging away at this program that we call discipleship. And, in the process, there is a massive transformation that goes on. That is the very thing that we recommit to in this Lenten journey. We emphasize the baptismal waters and we recommit to our Baptismal promises again for another year. Even though we only started our Lenten journey 10 days ago we probably need to acknowledge we have strayed in some way. We probably made lots of promises, just as in our diet program or an exercise program, and suddenly 10 days later, we find ourselves completely disappointed in our results because we have failed to do what we said we would do. We have not even gotten to the halfway point, and we know we have dropped off in our discipline.

That is why we come here each Sunday. We come to the table to be nourished, to recommit to discipleship and to be strengthened by seeing one another at the table as fellow members of the body of Christ. But we are also called to receive the body and blood of Christ so we can receive the strength of Christ. That is what Paul's letter to Timothy is about. Christ does not ask us to this transformation on our own. It is not some sort of long-term self-help program called discipleship. He gives us His grace through His Holy Spirit. He gives us the grace to live life to the fullest. That is how we truly transform. It is still hard work because we have to allow the grace of the Holy Spirit to work in our lives. We still have to choose to do the things we need to do and not choose to do the things that we should not do. That's where the hard work comes in.

So, today, as we continue our Lenten journey, let us make sure that we do not get disappointed or disheartened on our recommitments to our

Baptismal promises. Instead, may we continue to struggle and strive at being kind and gentle, at being encouraging to those who need it, at being forgiving to those who also need that from us, and in all things being loving to one another. Today, we choose to commit ourselves once again to this journey and we will experience the transfiguration of our lives, we will have a huge difference from the before to the after.

Embracing the Untouchable

It is one of the most difficult photographs I have ever seen; and yet, it is one of the most touching photographs I have ever seen. It is the picture of a man named Venicio Riva. Venicio suffers from a hereditary disease called neurofibromatosis, which leaves his body covered from head to toe in lesions and ulcerous lumps that look infectious. However, they are in fact not infectious but are grotesque and distorting.

Recently, Venicio visited St. Peter's Square and saw the Pope for the first time. The Pope, upon seeing him, without ever having known anything about him before, embraced him and kissed him on the forehead. Venicio has been suffering from this disease since he was 14 years old. He said that when most people see him the general reaction is repulsion. People turn and walk away. They are shocked. They think he is contagious, and they walk away. Instead, the Pope not only embraced him but kissed him. Venicio said that it was the first time in his life he felt like a human being

The Pope reached out to somebody who understood himself to be completely untouchable. In a sense, it is the same story that happens in today's Gospel. The Samaritan woman is not physically disfigured but in the eyes of the community, she was very much disfigured. She had five husbands and the one currently was not her husband. She was a woman and she was a Samaritan. All of those were three strikes against her, which is why Jesus should not have even spoken to her or gotten anywhere near her.

Instead, Jesus engages her in conversation. Remember the reason why she is at the well midday is because no other woman would go to the well with her. She was not allowed to go to the well with the rest of the women, so she was already segmented away from society. Yet, here is Jesus not only talking to her but engaging her in a deep dialogue about her life and about eternal life.

If we call ourselves Christian, then we are called to model ourselves after what Christ did today. The Pope has constantly challenged us to

41

reach out to people with mercy and with compassion first. Then ask questions later. The Pope has been consistent in his approach and each further image we get from him becomes equally more profound than the last. You and I are called to be that person who is merciful, who is compassionate and who is understanding.

Very few of us will ever come across that very rare genetic condition of an ulcerative body like Venicio Riva, and very few of us will come across somebody like the Samaritan woman, but we all have people in our lives that we choose to not have conversations with. For whatever reason—something they have said or done —they are now on the periphery of our lives and we deliberately keep them there. We are called, as Christians, to reach out; to be the mercy of Christ; to be the compassion of Christ.

That will be difficult for some of us because we will have to go beyond our political boundaries since that is where some of these people are. For others of us, we are going to have to shatter our religious boundaries. Still others of us, we will have to go beyond other boundaries, whether it be family, sexuality, or other matters; the list goes on and on…. Why do we put people on the outside of our lives?

The Pope is pleading with the whole Catholic Church, its clerical leadership and the laity to be people of compassion; to be people of mercy. He follows not his own steps. He follows the steps of Jesus Christ, who was first and foremost a person of love, mercy and compassion.

We are called to be those people. So, there is only one question that we need to ask ourselves this week: Who is on the outside of our lives —the periphery of our families —the periphery of our community? People we have cast there. How can we reach out to them in mercy and compassion and embrace them in spirit and in truth and welcome them into the grace of Christ?

Journey of Faith is a Process

After the 4-year-old's mother replied "No" on this third occasion to something the little girl wanted, the 4-year-old stomped in front of her mother and said, "I hate you. I hate you." She stormed off to her bedroom. Ten minutes later, she was back playing and talking with her Mom again. None of us would take those words seriously from a 4-year-old. We understand that a child is just having a tantrum.

On the other hand, if a 40-year-old woman went to her mother saying, "I hate you, I hate you," it would be a great difference. When we are children, we are not as aware of things. We do not understand the weight of that word. That word "hate" is a very severe word —even just repeating it as the child had said it, sounds so harsh. The child does not really understand what he or she is saying.

When we turn into our teenage years and then into our adult years, and into our mature adult years, we know the way things work. We become much more aware; we see things differently with more understanding. We are much more conscious of the power of words to do damage —the power of words to heal or to hurt. That sense of awareness or that sense of our eyes opening is something that comes with time. We come to see and understand life and how it is, and hopefully, that comes faster instead of slower. Sometimes, the struggle that parents have is their children do not come fast enough to those realizations and we tend to have a little more fighting.

In today's Gospel, we hear of a man who was born blind, who gets his sight not because he asks for it. This is John's Gospel. John's Gospel does not require faith for his miracles to work or as they are called in his Gospel, "signs." Jesus typically works with somebody who does not have faith. This is unlike the Synoptic Gospels in which faith is required before a miracle can work. In John's Gospel, they do not. In John's Gospel, faith comes after the sign. And so it does in today's Gospel.

The man is born blind —and while Jesus and the disciples walked by, the disciples ask, "Why is he blind? Was it because of the sins of his parents or his sins?" Jesus goes, "Neither." He goes over and puts a little spittle on the ground and heals him. The man didn't say, "Hey Jesus, heal me." He did not say in this Gospel "Hey Son of David, heal me." He didn't say anything. But notice what happens. The healed man slowly comes to faith. How? In the process of questioning. People questioning: "How did you get healed?" "It was that man." "How did you get healed again?" "I think he is a Prophet." How did you get healed again? "It is Jesus, the Lord." He went from man to Lord to the Messiah. "Who is this man that I should believe in and I will believe. Yes. I believe, my Lord." He comes to a deeper faith by questioning.

Often, we come to see our faith differently as we experience life, but we must enter into the questions. We must find a way to ask the questions because that is what brings us to deeper faith. We reach more mature and richer levels each time we ask questions. It is the journey we must go through which is what the blind man does. He receives grace and he builds upon that grace by cooperating and asking questions and so he comes to an even deeper faith.

If we are open to it, the Lord will show us more and more all the time, but we must be willing to ask. I would hate to have the same faith I had when I was only 4 years old. I would hate to have that same childish understanding of not only God but of the world still operating in my head. In that case, I would be saying a lot of silly things to a lot of people. I would be doing a lot of hurtful things. Sometimes, as Catholics, we seem to settle ourselves with a faith that was learned at 10 years old or 12 years old. Some of us "make" our Sacrament of Confirmation and we stop! I need to know no more! I'm done learning. Now I just practice.

That is not the faith journey. That is the beginning of faith. We need to continue to ask questions and work out that faith because we see differently; our eyes become opened as time passes. As we begin to see more, we then take more steps and do more things. It is only with that faith opened by eyes of faith do we come to the full realization of what we are called to do in faith for one another as a community.

A child who sees a homeless person does not fully understand how difficult that life could be for that person. I would hope as adults that we can look at a homeless person and have our heart bleed just a little bit and understand why and how that man was there. Why? Is there something I can do even though I do not fully understand why he is there? Before Christians distinguish themselves by what they do, they distinguish themselves by what they see. That is a mature faith. That is a faith that continues to grow. The older I get the more I realize how little I really know. That includes my faith but that is a mystery in God. I am not afraid to say that because I remain in Christ.

So today, like the blind man, we have been given grace upon grace so we keep on going back to God, asking more questions so that we can have a deeper and richer faith. We seek a more mature and adult faith because then we see with eyes of faith and our eyes are truly opened to follow Christ.

Life and Resurrection

One of the great privileges we priests have is to be able to journey with people on their last days. We get to be there in the most privileged, fragile and vulnerable moments of people's lives. We are called for anointing of the sick and finally when they are in the dying process of moving from this life into eternal life. There is a prayer called "The Prayer of the Commendation" which has some beautiful phrases in it like this… "Go forth from this world Christian soul. May the Lord meet you and welcome you into the garden of paradise. May He who is the Good Shepherd recognize you as one of His own." And then we say a few more words for them to passage from this life into the next.

From my many experiences of these moments and others, there is one thing that I am absolutely sure about in my ministry as a priest, and that is I have no doubt in eternal life. There are many things I have struggled with but resurrection I know is real. I have absolutely no doubt; not a single sinew or a muscle in my body disagrees. The reason for my certain belief is because I have watched so many people pass from this world into the next and I have been with them on that journey. I know it is for real because they testify by their actions and by their words of belief in God and being welcomed in that last section of the journey home. It is an absolute truth for me to believe in the resurrection and in Jesus Christ who claimed to be the resurrection.

In today's Gospel Jesus says, "I am the resurrection and I am the life. All who believe in me will not die." I am absolutely convinced that it is real. It is in large part why I have dedicated my life in service through the priesthood. It is not that I am flawless, or I think I am better than any other human being. I have flaws just like everyone else! But I have come to believe in the reality of Jesus and resurrection, and I want others to believe in that same message. It has transformed my life and I think it can transform others' lives. This is what Paul was trying to say in his letter to the Romans, that when you understand and believe in the resurrection your whole life is changed. We come to believe that and we come to live that reality in our lives and when we make mistakes, which we do regularly, when we sin, which we do regularly, we immediately pick ourselves up and turn back to the Lord and say, "Lord, I am sorry." We then go right back and face the Lord because the resurrection is for real. We are called to live that resurrection here and now, to live the joy of knowing that message with surety of heart and soul. Eternal life is our final destiny and that news gives our entire life context. We can truly live that joy of the Gospel that Jesus says today, "I am the resurrection and the life."

As we continue our Lenten Journey may we renew ourselves in that belief. May we assure ourselves in the resurrection. It is absolutely for real. However, let us not settle for just knowing it as some ethereal belief out there in some farfetched place but to recognize that it comes to inform us here and now, in our daily lives. So, when life sometimes throws us a curve ball and we are overwhelmed by lifes troubles; maybe by pain, or grief, or just the difficulties of life, that we put it in the larger context of eternal life. We will then see how small are the little things that upset us, how far away they are from where our final goal will be. It is not in any way to minimize the pain we are in or in any way to reject the reality of our current situation but to acknowledge it, in the light of eternal life, giving it the rightful context of a believer in Christ.

So today, may we renew ourselves by the joy of the Gospel and assure each other in our belief and knowledge in Christ as the one who is the life and the resurrection. Let us resolve to reform our lives and whatever mistakes and sins we have made, to leave them here at The Table of the Lord; to leave here renewed in that belief that Christ is the life. He is the resurrection and we have life in Him.

Time of Hope

Many years ago, in Northern England there was a cave-in in one of the coal mines in which twelve men were trapped inside. After the dust and debris settled, the leader of the group, in total darkness, called out to his twelve men and asked them to call out their name and give him their condition. All twelve men called out their names and reported back that no one had been hurt. After a few more moments, the leader of the group asked the timekeeper who was trained in such matters and for such disasters how much time do we have and what time is it now.

After lighting a match and examining the size of the space they were trapped in the timekeeper said, "It was 10:30 at the occurrence of the accident and assessing that we have 10 feet x 16 feet x 12 feet, I'd say we have two and one-half hours of time left." He quickly added some words of hope "It is plenty enough time if we all remain calm and we occasionally make a sound and one of us can be given that task. So, remain calm and we'll be fine." And he blew out the match.

And every so often, the leader would call out, "Time?" The timekeeper would report back that ten minutes had just passed or maybe fifteen minutes had passed and each time he added some words of hope and encouragement. Every so often the leader would call out again and no matter how long it was between the times, the timekeeper always seemed to answer 10 or 15 minutes. Just when they seemed to be grasping for air, the leader one more time asked, "How much time?" Once again he said, "Ten minutes and I believe I can hear the sound of the rescuers coming." Just then they all could hear the sound. Eventually, the rescuers punched a hole into their tiny cavern and lights filled in along with the needed oxygen.

After they rescued everyone, all but one survived. The one who did not survive was the timekeeper. After they carried his body out, they noticed clasped in his hand was his watch. The watch read 10:30, the occurrence of the accident. There was no timekeeping after all. All along he had helped them to remain calm. When the priest came and ministered to them, he said it was a miracle. You have been down there for six and one-half hours and it is unheard of that so many could last so long on so little oxygen. The one man, the timekeeper, had remained composed. He had kept his own fear internalized and instead ministered to the other eleven. This allowed them to remain calm and not panic and therefore not suck out the last portions of the oxygen left in that small cave. Instead he emptied himself of everything and ministered to these eleven men who survived.

It is very much the same image of what we hear today in the passion of Christ. For Christ "emptied Himself" as the second reading says in Paul's letter to the Philippians, "He emptied Himself to become a human," giving everything away so that we, as human beings, could know that in death, it is not the end. Jesus came to give us the hope of eternal life so we will know that our human existence is not the end. Christ ministers to us in the darkness of our lives, especially when we find ourselves in those last moments. But you will also notice what Jesus did, just like the timekeeper in the story, He died with dignity. He gathered His disciples around Him and ministered to them at a table that we sit around every Sunday. He ministered to them when He said, "Do this in memory of Me." He ministered to them recognizing that He needed to give them hope while maintaining His own dignity even to the moment of His last breath. But lest we think that the story of Jesus' passion is all warm and fuzzy, we know after listening to Matthew's recollection of His death that it is an extremely painful moment for Jesus. In His darkness even Jesus wanted to have the cup pass from Him; even Jesus wondered if our God had abandoned Him in His last moments.

So too for you and me, when we reach the darkness of our lives, we sometimes wonder if our God has abandoned us. We wonder if we could have the cup of pain pass us by. But we must also remember the end of the story that Christ also said, "Not My will but Your will be done;" that we give over ourselves to God the Father who will take us all to Himself even in our final moment.

So, in those moments when we may be in the midst of some pain and suffering ourselves, and we must endure with dignity some of that suffering, or we may be in the last moments of our life and we know that these are difficult days ahead. We take comfort in knowing that Christ is always with us. But it is probably more likely that we know someone else who is in darkness, who is cut off and in a cave. We must be willing to go and rescue them; we must be willing to go and dig them out and reach them, giving them the live giving oxygen of life and giving them hope.

There may be times when we are trapped right in there with them. We must minister to our parents who might be in the dying process or to a son or a daughter who is in a painful period of their life, or someone else we know who is struggling. But we must be like that timekeeper; we are called to hope and to remain calm. To know that life, life itself, is but a journey that will take us to eternal life.

Today, we recognize that Christ died for us and emptied Himself of everything so that we could know that even in the darkest movements of our life, the worst cave-ins of our life, He will come to rescue us and bring us the light of eternal life. In the end He will take us all to Himself for all eternity.

How Well We Have Loved

There is a TV show called "Undercover Boss." It is an interesting show where a boss in the organization, usually the CEO, goes undercover and pretends he is either an employee or seeking to be an employee. Then he discovers what his real employees are like and what their actual work is on the job. I recently saw one show about the CEO of a really large conglomerate company with lots of different divisions involved in very different types of companies.

One of the companies he had was a janitorial service, a very large janitorial division that does large contracts with the airports and all the major restaurants in Chicago and New York. He also had a shuttle service at the airport that takes people back and forth to the airlines with their luggage and to the car rentals.

There were two particular people that he interacted with during his undercover stay that touched me. One was a woman who came from one of the Eastern European countries. In this scenario the undercover boss was aspiring to be a janitor even though he was fairly overweight and in his mid-60's. God bless this woman because she was so kind to him. Even though he struggled to do the work, he did not do the work. There was one scene where he is cleaning the toilet bowl and he is absolutely dripping in sweat, so much so that it is dripping off him and into the bowl. The woman looks at him and says, "You are not doing it right." He looks at her and starts to get red in the face. She adds, "You know, you need to sit down; I think you're going to pass out." He sat back slouched against the wall as she proceeds to clean up what he had failed to clean up. She looks at him and says, "You know, you need to understand every toilet needs to be cleaned with the same attention; it doesn't make any difference whose toilet it is; every toilet is my toilet." The look on his face is shock; here he is dripping with sweat, completely frustrated, and he is getting a pep talk from his employee.

The other employee was a young man, a student, who was a driver shuttling back and forth to the airport. The undercover boss was once again a trainee, trying to drive the bus, get off the bus, get the bags, put the bags on the bus and get in and drive. I remember this one scene, he lifted a bag and a woman snapped, "Hey you! Take it easy with that bag; that's my bag." He looked at her and growled. He then got on the bus and started driving. Afterwards, the young man said to him, "Now, every customer is an important customer; you only have one interaction with them and one only. You grab their bags, put them up, be nice to them and maybe by the way you interact with them it will make their day a little bit better." Again, the look on his face was, "Wow." He was shocked because he didn't know he had such great people like this working for him.

The most touching scene of all was when he called them to the boss' office. Of course, they are nervous; they think they are going to get fired for something they had done so you could see that they were concerned. When the woman came in and saw him, she started crying and so did he. He had heard the story behind their lives and knew that the woman had to work two jobs. He was generous to her and then the young man comes in. He was an aspiring student who works for him and goes to school. He also helps and takes care of his mother who is an invalid. Again, the interaction was one of tears and consolation.

Afterwards he was interviewed and said it wasn't so much that he did not know he had such good employees, but what he did not know was the human element behind each one of them. He said, "Wow; they are really good people. They treated me so well. I was only an apprentice janitor and an apprentice taxi driver and yet they treated me as if I was special."

Today, we celebrate the Lord's Supper where He comes to us as a humble servant. He talks to us about the commandment to love one another and then He shows us what that means. He tells us to get down on our knees and wash the feet of one another. One must understand the context for Jesus to have done that for His disciples. He was their Lord, Master and Teacher. Washing feet was the lowest job in the household and was done by the youngest child in the household or the youngest and least of the slaves.

So, for Jesus to get down on His hands and knees to wash the feet of His disciples —Peter's reaction says it all, "No, you can't do that." Jesus said, "No. I must do this." This is what I mean by feeding my people: it is that we serve one another.

In other words, it is not what we do —whether we are a janitor or an executive, whether a teacher or a priest, whether it be a stay-at-home mom or a high-flying executive. It does not matter what we do, but how we do it. Jesus tells us what we are called to do is love one another. We do it because we care for the human being who is in front of us. We care for the Christ in one another.

You see, in the end, Christ is not going to judge us on our status in society; He will not judge us on the job we have; none of that will be a measurement on how we are judged. We will be judged on one thing, one thing alone: how we loved one another; not how well we lived but how well we loved.

So, this week as we go forth from here tonight, we celebrate the service of one another. There are people in all our lives that serve us, sometimes in humble ways. So, we need to recognize those people in our lives, whether it is our mothers, our fathers or some other person who humbly serves.

Number one, we need to recognize them and give them the dignity of being the human beings that they are. Number two, we need to practice at serving others. We need to be willing to don the towel and get down on our knees and wash the feet of somebody else.

Let's not make it just a symbol, let's make it a living symbol in our lives. May we respect and love one another because in the end that will be our only judgment, on how well we have loved.

Penalty Paid

One of the struggles I always have when I listen to the Passion of Christ is, "Why?" Why did God have to allow His Son to die? Why did God have to allow such a cruel and unusual death for His son? We are told it is for the sins of the world, our sins, yours and mine. That doesn't seem to settle my soul much and I struggle with it. I know that we are sinful, but I don't think that my sins or your sins are that radical, that grievous, that somebody, the Son of God, should suffer so much. Why such an unusual and painful death of our Savior?

The only way I can understand it is that God had a way in which He wanted to communicate something very powerful to us, that His justice and mercy meet. The best way I have been able to understand this is through a story. There once was a judge who was on the bench. One day a petty thief was brought before him. When he looked down from the bench, he recognized that it was his best friend from elementary school. He could hardly recognize the man because he was now disheveled, unkempt and messy looking but it was definitely him. He recognized who he was, right here before him in his own court. The thief had already admitted he had done the crime, so he was found guilty. The judge did not know what to do; he was truly guilty and even admitted it. He knew he had to give the punishment or penalty for the crime. With tears in his eyes, the judge cast judgment upon his best friend from school. He fined him $1,000, which was an appropriate penalty for the crime. Afterwards, he took off his robes, stepped down from the bench and went to the court clerk and wrote a personal check for $1,000. He gave his best friend a hug and said, "Go, and do no more evil."

I believe that is what God does for you and me. His justice says that our sins need punishment; there is a consequence for our sins; there is a consequence for all our sins, small or large and that is what He must do as a God of Justice. However, as a God of Mercy and a God of Love, He steps down from His heavenly throne and comes to us in the shape and person of Christ Jesus and He lays down His life in ransom and in payment for the very same penalty for all humanity's sins.

So, you see what this is all about is not suffering; it is all about God's love for us. His love is so overwhelming that He would give His most precious Son in payment for the penalty that He would mete out against us. As hard as that is for us to understand, Good Friday is all about God's love for you and me. That is what we must focus on. Yes, we must stop sinning as best we can, but we must know that we are loved by God through and through, that He loves us so incredibly that He would do such a thing for us. If that is the case, we understand why the power of His command is to "Love one another as I have loved you. Lay down your life for one another as I have laid down my life for you."

On Good Friday, we come to venerate the cross. As we come to receive the Body and Blood of Christ once again, I ask you to think about those people in our lives that we lay down our life for: our children, our parents, our friends. Also, ask the question how may I lie my life down for others. How can I love just a little bit more; how can I exert myself a little more? Yes, it is uncomfortable, but we need to push ourselves just a little bit more. Whether it is our parents, our children or our friends surely, we can love just a little bit more. Today, we are called to love, love, love; that is what Good Friday is all about.

Stay Awake!

The movie *Awakenings* tells a story of a doctor named Malcolm Sayer, who starts a new job at a mental hospital in the 1960's. It is a true story about how he comes to care for these patients. After a short time, he notices a pattern in a group of patients who seem to suffer all the same conditions. He discovers they have a condition called *encephalitis lethargica* that was known, at that time, as the "sleeping disease." In this sleeping disease, patients literally fall completely asleep, comatose in a catatonic state and are unresponsive in every way. Dr. Sayer ministers to them and tries to discover patterns in their behavior. In doing his research, the doctor discovers that a new drug called L-Dopa, which had been designed for treating Parkinson's disease, could have potential benefits for his patients. So, he ran a trial on one of these patients, Leonard Lowe, played by Robert DeNiro. Robin Williams, playing the part of Dr. Sayer, continues to prescribe heavier and heavier doses of the drug. Eventually this new drug wakes up Leonard and he is completely alive. Having been in this catatonic, sleeping state for nearly 30 years, Leonard wakes up into a world that he does not know.

As Leonard re-learns to live in this world, there is this phenomenal discovery of the value and the gift of life. During this process there is a bond that develops between the doctor, Malcolm Sayer and Leonard Lowe. Eventually, Dr. Sayer pleads with the benefactors of the hospital to give him enough money to put all 15 of the patients onto this medication. They do so and all 15 patients are given the medication. As a result, they all come out of their sleepiness and come alive. It is an incredible movie about how these people had lost decades of their lives, lost massive components of life itself and yet now they are alive and well. They enjoy life completely and value every single experience of life. Unfortunately, as time goes by, they discover that the drug wears off and the awakening is temporary. Eventually L-Dopa no longer works and they return to their catatonic state.

It is a painful movie to watch because the joy of life that they sought to enjoy and recapture is lost because the benefit of the drug does not last. All the doctors struggle to understand what has happened. Dr. Sayer gives this speech to the benefactors who have helped him finance the incredible high costs of this experiment and tells them, "Today we must face the reality of a miracle. We can hide behind a veil of science or we could say the drug has failed or that the patients could no longer handle the reality of having lost decades of their lives. But we do not know what went wrong any more than we know what went right to begin with." Then he adds, "There is one thing that we learned before this chemical window closed for them: there began another awakening, but this awakening continues past the chemical window, this awakening is the awakening of the human spirit." He said, "For the human spirit is stronger than any chemical, stronger than any dose of any pharmaceutical component. The human spirit is now opened for these people. With it, they have shown us the value of life, that the value of life is with family, with friends, with laughter, with the simple joys of being able to go out and enjoy the outdoors. These are the things that matter. These are the things we have forgotten. The simplest things."

The hospital unit is transformed because now the nurses and doctors tend to these patients, not as catatonic individuals without personality but as fellow human beings, who are hidden behind a state of sleepiness, fellow human beings trapped in illness.

I often wonder if we, as human beings, have sometimes experienced a spiritual sleepiness; that we occasionally wake ourselves up from this catatonic state and come to church on Sunday morning, only to fall right back asleep on Sunday evening. Or that we come here to these celebrations at Easter or Christmas and find it a wonderful awakening only to fall back asleep on Monday morning after Easter.

You see, my friends, this celebration today along with what the cross represents and what the resurrection represents, is not a temporary awakening; it is not a chemical awakening; it is for real. And a miracle exists in you and me. But we must be careful not to fall asleep, not to be overtaken by a spiritual sleepiness that can be cast over our society so easily, one in which we take the narcotics of society and put ourselves so quickly to sleep. We must resist the temptation of listening to the world that says sleepiness, spiritual sleepiness, is better than being fully alive in the Spirit.

Today, of all days, we come to celebrate that Spirit. We come to say the Spirit is alive in you and me; that Christ is risen among us today and we are to stay awake with Him. We are called to tend to that Spirit, to enliven that Spirit within us through prayer and works of charity. We do this so that we do not fall asleep tomorrow or on Monday and then come back again next Sunday to briefly awaken ourselves to a moment of spiritual reality. Instead, we come here each Sunday to stay awake, to stay awake in the Spirit of Christ, who is risen. Today, let us not pretend that we have taken some chemical that will awaken us for a moment, but instead realize that the same Spirit promised to the disciples is the same Spirit we hear about today. It is the same Spirit that is given to you and me. Christ is risen and He is alive in you and in me. Let us stay awake and tend to our spiritual self.

Loved and Lost Is Better Than No Love at All

There are many times in our lives when we experience the loss of a loved
one. It may be through death or through some form of betrayal or
infidelity. Sometimes, it is just the transition of a loved one out of our
lives through moving out of town or through a new job. Whatever
the painful losses in our own life, whenever they occur, the depth of
the pain can be so overwhelming, the darkness so incredibly deep
and painful that we wonder if we can ever overcome the depth of the
pain. It is especially true if we have lost one to death. We can be so
overwhelmed that we wonder if anything can overcome the pain, if
anything will get us past this time of darkness and loss. Yet, there is
a great irony in all this pain. The reason we experience such depth of
loss is because we have loved so much. In other words, if we did not
love the person and if we did not know the person through and through,
we would not experience any loss at all. There are lots of people who
die every day all around the world and it has no impact on any of us.
In reality, the size of the loss is directly proportional to the amount of
love that we feel for that person. The greater the love that we have, the
greater the loss that we feel.

In other words, death, loss and pain are direct functions of love; they are an
expression of love. I know it is a painful expression of love, but it is an
expression of love in our life. That is what we come to celebrate today;
that is the very thing that Easter is all about: LOVE.

In today's reading, we hear about how the two Mary's run to the tomb.
They go to the tomb because their loved one is gone; they go to the
tomb because the depth of their pain is so overwhelming that just
merely visiting the tomb will seem in some way to abate their pain.
They were not expecting a miracle; they were not expecting some
massive transformation. But what they saw was a miracle; what they
got was a complete transformation that would change their lives forever.
They experienced the loss but then they experienced resurrection. They
experienced exactly what Christ told them: that death could not take
away their love.

In other words, in Christ, this sting of death is lost. Yes, we do feel our loss, but we know that our love lives on. Christ assures us that because of the Resurrection our love never dies; death never separates us. Yes, we have the loss in the sense that we no longer physically have the person and we know, as anyone of us who has lost a loved one knows well, that the love never dies. We do not stop loving them because they are gone from our sight. Because we have loved them, we know we have lost something inside, but we know love goes on forever. Christ's message to the world is that very message of love: that despite the cross, despite death, love lives on forever.

If there is one thing I am completely sure of as a priest, it is the promise of the resurrection. I am absolutely convinced, without a single shadow of doubt, we will be given eternal life. The resurrection for all of us is real. Christ tells us if we want to participate in God then we must love one another; that is why Jesus gave us that single commandment because God is of love. God is love. Therefore, when we love somebody, we are participating in God's very self. That is the greatest gift that we can have, love. It is that message that Jesus comes to give us today. The Resurrection promises us that our love never dies. So, whenever we experience a loss, in whatever form that may be, we are called to continue to love others, to continue to express that love for others because we are called to continue that life that God and Christ put within us.

Now that sounds great and in theory it is wonderful but when we have lost a loved one, it is very hard. When we experience what the Marys experienced in today's Gospel, we experience such a depth of pitiful darkness and pain that it is sometimes hard to live with and sometimes hard to believe in the Resurrection. Sometimes we wonder how or why God allows such pain. But we now know it is directly related to our love. The only way out of that darkness is to do exactly what we have done with the loved one that has left us: that is to love again, to love somebody else. It does not take away from the love we have for our loved one, but it means that we continue to love because that is the love that will never die in the end. The Resurrection promises us that we will be reunited with all our loved ones and all that love will continue in God because all things exist, and all things live in God.

This week, if we are remembering a loved one that we have lost and we are struggling with that darkness, be assured of the sure and certain knowledge that Christ is Risen and the Resurrection is real. Today, we celebrate the gift of love and in that love, we know that God assures us that our love never dies. That is the message of the resurrection: to love is to live the resurrection here and now. We must live the resurrection in our lives. We must love one another despite the inevitable pain of loss. Today, we will continue to exercise the commandment from Christ in our own life, to continue to love one another and so continue to live in God and live in the Risen Christ.

I Cannot Believe It!

I cannot believe it! I cannot believe I've finally made it! I cannot believe I'm actually here! I cannot believe this is actually happening to me! I cannot believe that the Lord would allow this to happen to me! These are some of the different phrases we use when good things and bad things happen to us. When we arrive at the place of our dreams that for years we have always wanted to be we say, "I cannot believe I'm finally here; I am standing over the City I have always wanted to see." Or on graduation day, we say, "I cannot believe I've finally done it. I've made it." Or if we have a new job, we say, "I can't believe I have the job I've always wanted. I cannot believe this is happening. Is this real?"

Or, if we have something bad happen, we say, "I cannot believe this is happening to me. All that I have done; how can the Lord allow this to happen to me? I cannot believe this right now." Yes, these are some of the things we say when we have reached certain milestones, special events or places in our life or when things happen to us in a negative way.

Now, most often, we attribute all the negative things to God. "Why is God allowing this to happen to me?" And when they are good things, we seem to quite readily take the credit for them by saying, "Oh, I cannot believe *I've* made it! I've done it!" But when it is something negative, we say, "I cannot believe *God* is allowing this to happen!"

In today's Gospel, we hear to a certain extent those same words from Thomas when he says, I cannot believe, or I won't believe it until I see it. But then when he sees the Lord, he does something that few of us ever allow to happen. He really believes. He puts aside his doubt completely and says, "My Lord and my God." He does not look to anyone else. He just says, "My Lord and my God" and really believes. Thomas is remembered for "doubting" but we should remember him more for truly "believing."

The challenge in our lives is that when good things happen to us, we don't ascribe them to God. When things are going well in our lives, we seem ready to take credit ourselves. When things are going well and good things are happening to us, do we say, "Lord, thank you for the gift of this easy part of my journey in life." It is a real challenge because when things are going well, we seem to forget about where God is in our life. And that is the reason our church is so often empty because things are going so well for everybody. I don't want things to change for people, but I do wish they would recognize their God in their lives.

I don't know about you, but when things are not going so well, I often end up back at my prayer desk. When things are not going so well, I come back to the church in a more powerful way. I know of my need for God when things are not going well. But when things are going well there is a temptation to forget to be grateful to God.

When Thomas saw, he believed. We too are called to see and believe. But oftentimes, you and I, even when we do see, we do not believe; even when we see the powerful hand of God in our own life, we still do not believe that God is a part of it –that's the temptation.

The challenge for us is to look again at our lives; to look at what is going on in our lives and see the wonderful things that are happening; to see with eyes of faith and to see our God at work, and to say, "My Lord and my God." That is our challenge today. To look at our children and see how good they are; how good it is to have a job; how good it is to have a house; how good it is to have a community around us; how good it is to have a family that cares for us. Not that all the above are perfect. They are not, but they are God's gifts to us; God is in the midst of all of it. Today, may we look again at our lives and see the God who is present; and like Thomas, let us see and believe and cry out, "My Lord and my God."

Technique of Discipleship

Recently, I was hiking, and I met a young boy and an older woman, who could have been his mother but was most definitely a personal trainer. She was teaching the young boy how to be a better runner; she was describing how to keep his chest upright and shoulders back, swing those arms high and pull them back fast to gain momentum, to keep stride long and get the toe out all the way. You could see that the boy was practicing exactly what his personal trainer was teaching him. Her instructions were very technical and exact. Clearly, she knew what she was talking about.

They were traveling in the same direction I was, so I was able to see his trainer in action and his practice of her advice. They would do a little bit and then practice it. This went on for about four miles or so. By the time he got to the end, he was running more confidently with a smoother gait and definitely a more correct way to run. I suspect he was a runner; they were both great runners but here he was practicing getting even better. It is not as if he did not know how to run. It is natural for all of us to know how to run. But what he was learning was the technique of running really well; learning the technique to getting the best and the most out of each and every stride. I don't know whether he was willing or unwilling, but he was definitely getting better by the end of the four miles.

In today's Gospel that is exactly what Jesus does to the disciples; He teaches them how to be disciples. He demonstrates to them how to be disciples and how it is technique that is important. Jesus was always about showing His disciples how to be disciples but today, and during all the Resurrection accounts, we hear instructions of how to be a disciple. He is teaching His disciples about being a disciple when He was no longer around in the flesh. He was demonstrating how to be a disciple when He was not around. Let's take a look at the exact technique He shows us today.

He first comes alongside those who are journeying and listens to their story. He does not start out in any way talking about Himself; He listens to their story first. After He has heard all their story, he connects their story with scripture and connects their story with God's story through scripture. He then breaks bread, the Eucharist, and vanishes.

That is the model of ministry to which we are called. We need to note that these were not the apostles that He appears to, but ordinary disciples. In other words, this is not about how to do professional model of ministry, but it is for every single disciple. We are all called to follow that technique of discipleship which we call evangelization; we go to proclaim the Gospel to others through our actions.

Let's look a little more closely at the model and technique. He does not go out by proclaiming first. He doesn't go out and tell them to come to the Eucharist first. He does it by first listening to their story. So, for us, that is what we are called to do. We are called to listen to the story of those around us, most especially our young adults and youth who are struggling greatly with understanding our faith, who struggle greatly with the pressures of the world to not believe because the world tells them that there is nothing to believe in. We need to listen to their story first and then we can connect them to what we know in our faith, through scripture and through tradition. We connect these stories to their story and only then, we invite them to Eucharist, to the table and break bread with them.

This is what we are called to be as disciples and ministers, but it does not stop there. Do you notice what happens in today's scripture? What happened when Jesus broke the bread? He vanished. You might ask, "Well, where did He vanish to or what happened?" We believe that He did not vanish in the sense of disappearing; He vanished in the sense of their sight. In the breaking of the bread, they became Christ. He promised to be there every time they celebrated the breaking of the bread and drinking of the wine. He becomes the bread broken for others. He becomes the wine poured out for us. In other words, they become His living presence in the world. Realizing that, they leave Emmaus and run back to Jerusalem to proclaim the word that they have witnessed to all who will hear.

That is what we are called to do when we celebrate at this table; we start that cycle of life again. We become the Christ and go forward to listen to other people's stories, to connect it back to scripture and to our tradition and then to invite them back to the table once again. That is the cycle of discipleship. It is the model that Christ is showing all of us to be that example for others and to do so with joy. We do not do it out of some sort of painful obligation. We do it according to scripture with joy in our hearts; we go forward from our Jerusalem here and go forth to proclaim it in the world by our action. So today we celebrate the gift of Christ among us once again in the bread and in the wine. We not only come to renew ourselves at this table, but we also come to model ourselves on his technique of being a disciple. Most especially, to listen to our youth and young adults who may be dealing with the struggles and demons within their own lives.

We listen to their stories and attempt to connect their story to our own tradition and scripture, and finally, we come to the table to be renewed and to break bread together.

Today, we renew ourselves in that Christ; we become that Christ once again so that we can continue the model of discipleship that He sets before us.

We are the Shepherd and the Gate

We know people in different ways and in different capacities. Some people we know as our parents, children, siblings, uncles, aunts or other different relatives. We know doctors, nurses, patients and the list goes on and on. We know people in different ways because we have different relationships with them in different capacities. But the common thread between all these relationships is that there are set expectations or set values attached to these relationships. In other words, there is a set understanding of what the values and expectations are.

Today, we hear of a relationship that we are called to have. Jesus says that He is the Shepherd and you and I, we, are the sheep. I don't know about you but that does not sound very nice! If you think about it – it does not sound very nice—to be a sheep. But that is probably because our understanding of what a shepherd is and what the relationship is with his sheep is very limited. What we know today about shepherds is that they have dogs that corral their sheep together; they bring them back in, let them roam on the hills, and then bring them back to the farm or to the ranch. Today, the shepherd does not sleep with the sheep; he doesn't stay with them; he comes back to his own house and goes out and gets his dogs to bring the sheep back to him when needed. In ancient times, the shepherd had a very different relationship with the sheep. A shepherd back then had a small flock of sheep and he would know his sheep by name. He would name each of his sheep, much the same way we name our pets. The sheep were not pets, but he would know them so well that he would call each by a name, and they would recognize his voice. If a sheep became hurt in any way, the shepherd would tend to that wound immediately. Remember also that most of them were nomadic people so they were on the walk all the time and therefore he would sleep with the sheep. If a sheep became lost, he would corral his sheep and go and seek to find the lost sheep. That was the expectation. That was the understanding of what the shepherd does.

So today, we hear that Jesus is the Good Shepherd and we are the sheep. What He is saying to us is that He knows you and me by name, and that when He calls us, we ought to know His voice. When we are hurt, He will come and tend to us; when we are lost, He will come to seek us out and find us. That is the kind of relationship that Jesus is trying to get across in this passage. That He is the shepherd who will care for His flock.

But there is another thing that He says here that might be a little strange – that He is the gate. And again, if we do not understand ancient times, we also would not understand this. The gate was not like a metal gate. You see, they were nomadic tribes and traveled from place to place. In each of these places where they would shelter, there was what is called a sheepfold. It was a walled-in area with an opening at the front. Through that opening, all the different shepherds would bring all their sheep inside. All the different sheep would be mixed in together. When it was time to leave, the shepherd would call out their names and all the sheep would follow that shepherd out.

There was a wall all the way around the sides with one opening or entrance. At night the shepherds would sleep at the entrance called the gate. If there was only one shepherd with sheep in that sheepfold, he would lay full length across the gate to protect the sheep and to guard against anyone trying to come in to steal the sheep, or to keep them from wandering out. Jesus protects and cares for his fold, His sheep, and His disciples. He will always protect us in the dark of night and in the darkness of our lives. He will not let any harm come to us and ensures we do not wander away.

The challenge is that He is both the shepherd and the gate to us. He promises to care for us, to seek us out when we are lost and to protect us when we are in times of darkness. All that sounds wonderful, but what does that really mean to you and me today? Well, it means that if we call ourselves Christians, we are to model our lives after Christ which means that you and I are called to go out and take care of the hurting sheep among us. You and I are called to go forward and to seek the lost sheep among us. You and I are called to protect the fold against people who would have us dispersed and otherwise. We must act as a shepherd and a gate to one another. We must be mindful that the fold we are part of is not just our immediate family. Our fold is also that of our larger Christian community. We are called to care for all those who are hurting; all those who are lost. We are called to reach out to the jobless, the under-employed, and the people who are on the streets. We have a purpose. Our purpose is to be like the Good Shepherd and to reach out to those who are hurt, and to protect them as best we can.

So, today as we leave here nourished at the table of our Lord, we also come away strengthened to be the Good Shepherd and the gate to others; to seek those who are hurt and to tend to them; to seek those who are lost and try to bring them back to the fold; to seek those who are in darkness and in the night of their life and to protect them. We are called to be the Good Shepherd. We are called to be the gate.

Oxymoron

I am sure most of you have heard the term "oxymoron". Oxymoron refers
to a figure-of-speech that puts two apparently contradictory terms
together. I know that some of us can think of some obviously funny
ones. For example, there is an "open secret", which is an oxymoron;
or a "dark light" or "jumbo shrimp". And then of course there are the
other ones that are funnier such as "government intelligence" or "honest
politician".

In today's reading, we hear of an oxymoron that is very powerful. We
must stop and listen for a moment to truly understand what is being
said to the early disciples. The phrase "living stones" is an oxymoron.
If something is living it is dynamic, alive and ever growing. A stone on
the other hand is something that is permanent or lifeless; it is something
that is stable and maybe even immoveable. Yet both things have been
put together and you and I are called to be "living stones." How are we
to understand that we are called to be living stones?

First, we have to unpack this figure of speech a little bit. Jesus Christ is
"the" living stone and He is also the cornerstone on which all is to be
built. Therein lies the key to unlocking this scripture passage —we are
called to be the living stone as in living and dynamic and we are called
to be spiritually based in the foundation of Jesus Christ. He is meant
to be our roots and our stability. He is immovable. This is what the
scripture quotes from the Old Testament today: we are always about
Jesus Christ, the foundation, the cornerstone.

You and I are called to be that living reality. Just as the early Christians
looked at the signs of the times, we are called to do the same thing and
look at the signs of our times. We are called to be living and organic and
yet at the same time to be the solid immovable reality of Christ Jesus.

In today's first reading the early Christians had to figure it out because
they initially thought that the message of Jesus was only for the Jews.
Then they realized the Spirit was now coming to the Gentiles or the
Hellenists as the ancient people called them. So, we are also called, like

them, to recognize the signs of the times and see where God is calling us. For them, they recognized that God was calling them to the entire world. They now understood that they had to change their ways of being to adapt and recognize that they were to be the people for all nations. We, in our own time, must do the same thing.

Today, we come to celebrate the Eucharist. We are doing something that every one of us has done before but we have to recognize that it is the same church and yet it is a very different church that we are in today. Another oxymoron– it is the same church, but it is also different. What is the same is that we celebrate the same Eucharist. What is different about this church today is that this current society is different from the society of the previous generation which was different from the generation before that. Each one of us must adapt to the society in which we live here and now. It is the same but different.

We have come to celebrate the Body and Blood of Christ that we receive at this table. But we are called to live that reality in the ordinary world. No matter what our vocation in life, whether we are lay people or in the religious life, each one of us is a unique component of our church.

Every single one of us is different and yet the same. We are different because each one of us has a different gift; we are the same because each one of us is a child of God. Every one of us is called to be fully different and yet be the same child of God. Each one of us has unique gifts and we are called to use these gifts to be that living stone, to be alive and to do the best we possibly can in every way.

But the one very important oxymoron we celebrate every single time we come to this Eucharist is Jesus Christ himself because He came and He said, "I am risen from the dead!" That is the greatest oxymoron of all time: risen dead person. How could we celebrate the risen Christ who is dead? But that is exactly what we do at this table. It is very important that you understand what we celebrate here —that when we come to receive the Body and Blood of Christ, we believe we become what we receive; we become the living Body of Christ for others; we become the living Blood of Christ for others.

What we celebrate here today is that we become the living stones. We are called to be the living Christ to others. We are called to become people who are fully human, people who are kind, gentle, patient as well as loving and forgiving. Those cannot be just words; these are actions that require great work. All of us who come here often know how hard that work is and that is why we continue to come back to the table because we need to continue to be nourished; to continue to live the reality of that stone that comes alive in society.

Every one of us is called to be the living Christ, the living stone in the world. Together we come to celebrate and receive the nourishment to be able to change this world with our lives. We strive to be the best we can be so that all of us together can be the living stones of the people of God, the Body of Christ.

God's Little Helpers

Fred Rogers, or "Mister Rogers," as we have known him for over five generations, wrote a memoir in 2002 about the impact of his mother's wisdom on his life. "When I was a little child, I used to watch television and sometimes I would see all sorts of scary things happening around the world. My mother would always say, 'Look for the helpers; you will always see helpers in the midst of any disaster or calamity.'" He reflected about it later in his memoir saying how he always remembered those words in times of personal, national or even international disasters. He would look upon any difficult situation and was always able to see helpers or as he says in his memoir, "I was always astounded at how many helpers, how many people care in moments of disaster and tragedy."

Mrs. Rogers gave her young son, Fred, a great gift and it was not just a gift of wisdom, it was a gift of faith and a gift of hope. Mrs. Rogers speaks about, what we as Christians call, Hope. That is exactly the same thing the letter of Peter speaks of today. No matter what happens, God is always with us. Mrs. Rogers demonstrates this hope by those helpers who are always willing to step in to help, care and love. When we think about all the disasters around the world, the different wars and tragedies that occur, there are always people helping; there are always people trying to turn it all around, to make good out of even the worst situations.

Tomorrow we celebrate Memorial Day and we recognize those men and women who literally laid down their lives for the freedom and defense of our country. They are those helpers in the worst of times for our country. Think for a moment of 9/11 for example. How many of our firefighters and police just stormed into that building to do what they could do, laying down their own lives to help others. Later, how many more families came to tend to those firefighters' families in their loss. Yes, there are lots of helpers in the midst of tragedies.

Something a little bit closer in our own history is the Tsunami in Japan. We saw how many helpers came to reach out to them in their time of need.

73

Even then, many huddled together often not knowing what to do but at the very least trying to help one another. More recently we had tornados in our own country. Again, how many helpers: police, firefighters, ambulance drivers and so many more neighbors just bundling together to be the helping hands, the helpers and caregivers of this world.

We may also think of some of our own personal tragedies that may have happened to us in our own lives. How many people have reached out to us in our time of need? Maybe it was something as simple as a small illness or maybe something even more devastating as a death of a loved one. People reached out to us and that is evidence that our God is present, evidence of our belief, our core belief in the Christian Hope.

Today's reading reminds us of that Christian Hope. The Letter of Peter reminds his readers that when people challenge their faith and ask in the midst of their tragedies why do they believe, the reason they choose to believe is because God is present in all of it. He further reminds them they must demonstrate it with gentleness, reverence and with joy in their hearts. We too are challenged to the same standard. We must continue to believe in that same Christian hope and know that God is always there. Sometimes it is difficult because help does not seem to come fast enough. But it is more than just recognizing the help of God through other people's hands; we must also be willing to be the helpers to others in need. When we come to the table each Sunday, we promise to become that body broken for others; we promise to become that blood of Christ poured out for others; we promise to become God's helpers, God's little helpers in the world. We promise to demonstrate to others that God is present to them and that Christian Hope is real.

But there are many other ways in which we can do so. There are many other little ways in which we can become God's little helpers in our own community. Right here, in this house today, there are many people who are in need of that ray of hope, who are in need of that helping hand, that smile, that gentle cheer, that peace and joy to believe that God is really here in our midst. You and I are called to be that helper. It could be something as simple as reaching out and making a phone call. It could be something as simple as reaching out to the person next to you and asking them how they are and listening to them. It could be something as simple as a parent sitting down with their child and helping them do their homework or listening to their woes of school. There are many, many ways in which we can be God's helper.

It can be far away, near at hand, or right here in the midst of us. The one thing we are called to do is to look at every opportunity, every single disaster, misfortune, or personal tragedy as an opportunity for us to be God's little helper, God's hands and feet to those in need. So today, as we go forth from having celebrated at the table of the Lord, having received the Body and Blood of Christ, we are called to go forth from here to be the Body and Blood of Christ. We choose to demonstrate our commitment of the Gospel, to love one another by being God's little helper.

Witness What We See

"Be witnesses to the Gospel." When one thinks of the term "witness" there are certain expectations. If I asked you to be a witness to a car accident, for example, you would, at the very least, have had to be there. Secondly, we expect you would have seen the accident. One can be at an accident and still not be a witness because one could say, "I didn't see what happened." You turned your eye away for just a second or maybe you simply were not paying attention. So being a witness requires literally that you be there, to see first-hand what happened and then to take note of what happened.

But is that all there is to be a witness? A witness usually requires one to tell what has happened. It is not enough to have been there and seen it, but one must be willing to give testimony to what one has witnessed. There are three different components. Being there, seeing and testifying to what one sees. As often happens, there are situations that occur and there can be many completely different versions of what happened. Why? Because we all see what has happened slightly differently; we all see with our own unique perspective, if you would, or maybe we were just not paying attention.

Today, we are called to be witnesses of Christ, the Risen Christ. I ask you, how are we to be witnesses to the Risen Christ if we have never seen Him firsthand? It is a question we need to grapple with; how can we lay claim to witness Christ whom we have not seen? The disciples have seen him; we have not. So then, since we are called to be witnesses, how can we be witnesses? I would submit to you that the only way we can is to see with different eyes; we must see with eyes of faith. When we see with eyes of faith, we can really see God in our lives, and we can lay claim and be witnesses to that reality.

Therefore, part of what we have to do is to be honest. Today's Gospel tells us that the disciples were eyewitnesses; they were literally there. They saw, they believed but they doubted. Now here we have the actual disciples and still they struggled and doubted. This often happens to us so we must be willing to look with eyes of faith, to look at life and to see God. We need to be able to say: "I am doubting because I cannot see where God is operating, not that God isn't here but that I just do not see God right now."

I know that sounds like a very small difference, but it is actually a huge difference and one of the biggest struggles our young adults and our youth have with us. When we are not honest in our faith journey, when we are not honest and share where we struggle with our faith, when we do not share our doubts with our children and our youth and young adults, then they think it is all a little bit too pious; it's all a little bit unbelievable. But if we are honest, we know that we have all been through some dark periods in our life where some stuff happened to us and we just don't see where God is. But in the midst of all that pain and darkness, we still have to choose to believe even when we cannot see.

Like the apostles, we doubt, but that is okay. We still choose to believe even though we doubt. That is what our young adults need to hear. They need to hear that you and I have had those ordinary struggles and that there have been times in our lives where we just didn't get it. We wonder where our God is, and we struggle. Yet, we still choose to believe in our God. It is not enough to be there; we need to look again with eyes of faith; we need to look at what is going on in our life and not to question "if" God but "where" God is in the midst of all this. And if there is darkness we need to say, "I know God is here; I may not see it right now, but I wonder where our God is." When we realize it, then we lay claim to that reality and we acknowledge it.

Now where our young adults and our youth really struggle is when we lay claim to believe but then we are unkind, we are impatient, and oftentimes unforgiving. Frustrated, they say, "Oh, okay this doesn't make sense at all now. You claim to believe, and you want to teach the teachings of the church of being forgiving and being loving and yet you don't do that?" Consequently, the young adults and youth reply, "Na!" and they walk away from Church. So, we need to take ownership of the struggle of our faith and of the struggle of practicing our faith because it is hard work. We must choose to see with eyes of faith and then we will see and recognize where God is in our lives. Then witness with our lives with everything we say and do. The disciples found it hard and so will we. That is why we come to the table each week: to receive strength not only from the Lord directly in the bread and wine now made into the Body and Blood of Christ, but also from each other. We must be honest in our journey and that just like the disciples, we see, we believe but we doubt. Today, we come to the table to be renewed in the Ascended Christ Jesus and we choose to believe once again. To lay claim to what we see and choose to testify and to share the witness of Christ in our life. Today, we come to see, believe and to witness to what we see and believe.

Eat, Shoots and Leaves

In her book called "Eat, Shoots and Leaves," BBC Radio host Lynne Truss talks about the power of grammar and how important it is to hold onto the English grammar. She illustrates her thesis by telling an anecdotal story about how a Panda walks into a bar, has a drink and some food, finishes the food, takes out a gun, shoots the bartender and walks out. The people are stunned and ask the panda, "Why did you do that?" The panda turns around and throws a book of grammar over his shoulder and says, "I'm a Panda. Look it up."

So, the waiter looks up the definition of Panda in the book and it says, "A large black and white mammal, originally from China. Eats shoots and leaves." The intention is to illustrate the power of a simple comma. That the Panda eats shoots and leaves as opposed to eats, shoots and leaves. The comma, the punctuation, makes all the difference.

Today, we celebrate the feast day of the Holy Spirit, the feast day of our parish and indeed the feast day of the entire Church. We celebrate that the Holy Spirit, if you would, is the punctuation in our life that makes all the difference. If rightly used punctuation can transform any sentence. So too with the Holy Spirit, if rightly used, it can transform our lives completely. But just like good grammar, it needs to be used to have its effects.

We, as Catholics, are almost *afraid* of the Holy Spirit. We are not so much afraid of what the Holy Spirit will not do but afraid of what it might do. It might make us alive. It might make us alive like those Pentecostals. Praise Jesus! Yeah. We need not be afraid of the Holy Spirit. The Holy Spirit is, as the Acts of the Apostles says today, that fire —it talks about the fire that comes to us, that lights us up and impels us to go forward and to do what needs to be done. So, we must allow the Holy Spirit into our lives.

Now we are all given gifts, different gifts but as the letter to the Corinthians talks about today, we are animated by the same Spirit. Also, the letter says we must recognize and use those gifts we are given for the good of all. Yet, we must be willing to allow the Spirit to work in our life; we need to cooperate with the Holy Spirit. We have to use the punctuation in our lives. It can make all the difference to our life. Sometimes that punctuation looks like a comma, where we pause before we move on to something else. Sometimes, it is a period where we stop what we are doing before we can start something new. There are other times when it is a dash —a long pause, before we move on to the rest of the sentence of our life. Or maybe it is a semicolon; a little more than a little pause, but a pause where we must reflect on what will soon happen in our lives. Then there are times when it is a full colon in our lives: we stop and make a deliberate move into the next stage in our life. Then there are times we need a new paragraph; maybe, it is going off to high school, college, or a new job. Still other times it is an exclamation point. A word of thanksgiving, a word of gratitude or awe! At other times it is a question mark when we must pause and ask the question, "Where do I go from here?" You see as Catholic Christians, we do believe the Holy Spirit is the punctuation in our life but just like good grammar, we must use it.

So, today as we celebrate our own feast day here, and the feast day of our Church, the gift of the Holy Spirit has been given to every single one of us; as Paul says, each in our own way. Each manifested for the common good; for the good of all. Today, may we have a long pause, may we take a semicolon; pause and reflect of our own lives. Or maybe ask the question, where are we today?

Yes, on this feast of Pentecost, we are called to punctuate our lives with the gift of the Holy Spirit. Today, it is appropriate as we celebrate Mother's Day in the USA, maybe we can make an exclamation point to those mothers who have served us for so many years. For those moms who have given so much love to us, to recognize that gift and to offer thanks to God and not to be afraid to pause, and then say, Happy Mother's Day. Thanks!

Fabric of the Soul

There is a story told of a poor jeweler, who was wrongly convicted and imprisoned for a crime he never committed. He was imprisoned in the local city jail that was one of the fortresses of that region. One day his wife came to visit and pleaded with the guards saying her husband was a devout man and needed his prayer rug. She gave them his prayer rug and they gave it to the jeweler.

So, five times every day, the poor jeweler would roll out his prayer rug and pray to his God putting his face down to the rug as it was his custom. He did it day after day after day.

After many months, he became frustrated and bored in prison, so he asked the prison guards, "Look I'm a jeweler; I'm used to doing something with my hands all the time; let me do something for you. Give me some old scraps of metal and some precious stones and I'll fix it up and make jewelry. Then you can sell it at the local bazaar and make money for yourselves." The guards immediately agreed to this lucrative arrangement. Each day they brought him scrap pieces of metal and pieces of old jewelry and he worked all day. By the end of each day, he would produce different pieces of beautiful jewelry. This went on for many months and the guards made lots of money. They were very happy with this arrangement.

Then one morning the guards went to his cell and he was gone. His door was locked but the old jeweler was nowhere to be seen. A couple of weeks later, they caught the person who had done the original crime, convicted him and put him away. One day while the guards were in the local square at the bazaar, they saw the old jeweler selling his wares. They immediately went to him. When he saw them, he was fearful for his life, but they assured him, "Oh no, no. We know you were innocent. We have the right person now, but we have a question. We have the finest jail in all the surrounding region; how did you escape without opening the door?" He said, "Well, now that I know that I am free and I'm safe, I'll tell you. When my wife knew that I was wrongly imprisoned, she went to the architect of the prison and begged for the blueprint. She got the blueprint and for many months, she wove the blueprint into the prayer rug so that it was hidden in the fabric of the prayer rug. Every day I put my face into that prayer rug and I studied every square inch of the plans of this place. It also contained the combination for every lock in the entire garrison. So every day you brought me metal, I made you jewelry and I made myself keys. And when I had made my keys for every door, I walked out."

Now, I know that is a funny story and you may ask, "What on earth does that have to do with Trinity Sunday?" I think this is like our own lives: God weaves into the fabric of who we are the hidden key to everything in our lives. He weaves into the fabric of who we are the story of what we need in our life; everything we have is within us. He puts his very Spirit inside of our hearts. Like the poor jeweler we have to put our face to the prayer rug; to study clearly what is the design God has put within us so that we can understand it and set ourselves free to live in this world. Now again, that sounds wonderful but how do we go about doing it? I don't know any other advice to give you other than to spend time praying. We, like the poor jeweler, must find some time to pray; to listen and reflect upon God's creation and on our own lives.

I know it sounds easy but all of us find it so hard to get the time to pray. But I do not know how else we can come to know God's design and God's plan unless we are willing to take the time and reflect upon our own lives. When we take time each day and look at what is going on in our lives, we look at the troubles, the joys, the sorrows, the woes and all the different things that happen, when we stand back and look at them, we start to see God's hand and God's fingerprints in what is happening.

It sometimes takes us a long time to figure it out and sometimes it is very hard to figure out, but God's plan is there. Like the pattern woven in the fabric of that prayer rug, so too, is God's plan woven into our lives. If we keep looking at it, I am absolutely convinced we will see it. The great celebration that we have today is the mystery of the Holy Trinity. While it is wonderful to say Father, Son and Holy Spirit, three Persons in one God, we must be very careful because even just trying to say that; we are in some way trying to say what is indescribable. It is impossible to encapsulate into words who God is. One thing we can know about God comes from scripture. It says, "If we want to come to know God then we love. When we love one another then we participate in God's very self and that is how we know God."

There is a great Italian priest of the 19th century who used to say, "We ought not to look for God out in the stars and in the world beyond, but all we have to do is to look for the God who is within us, a guest of every soul and there He lies. Therefore, if you want to understand God in concepts, it is impossible but that to understand God in love, it is possible." It is a great quote because it comes back to the cornerstone of who we are as Christians, that when we love one another, we are participating in God. It is my firm conviction that if we can reflect and be honest in our lives, when we look at our own lives, we will see our own weaknesses; we will see what we do and how often we fail. When we do that, we can go back into our day and be a little bit more humble, recognizing that I am not much different myself and I can now love this person a little more because I have my own weaknesses and my own strengths.

So today, as we celebrate the Most Holy Trinity, it is wonderful to enter into intellectual thought and try to understand God. I encourage you to not only do that but to also reflect upon how God is woven into the fabric of our own souls and how we are called to know God by loving others. And as a result, when we do this, we participate in the mystery of the Trinity.

We Receive What We Are—The Body of Christ

"Because the loaf of bread is one, we, though many we are, are one body for we all partake of the one loaf" (1 Cor. 10:17)

A pastor in a country parish heard that one of his parishioners was going about announcing that he would no longer attend Mass. His rebellious parishioner was advancing the familiar argument that he could communicate just as easily with God out in the fields with nature as in the Church building on Sundays.

One winter evening the pastor called on this reluctant member of his flock for a friendly visit. The two men sat before the fireplace making small talk, but carefully avoiding the issue of church attendance. After some time, the pastor took the tongs from the rack next to the fireplace and pulled a single coal from the fire. He placed the glowing ember on the hearth.

The two men watched as the coal quickly ceased burning and turned ashen gray while the other coals in the fire continued to burn brightly. The pastor remained silent. Then after a few minutes the parishioner said "Father, I'll be at Mass next Sunday."

I believe we are the coals in the fire. We need each other to keep burning brightly. If we fall outside the community for any reason we often stop burning brightly and turn ashen gray. For us here, we are all members of the community of Holy Spirit and indeed members of the larger Catholic Church. One of the most common ways of referring to our community, to the people of God, has been as the Body of Christ. Yes, we are all members of the same body, the Body of Christ. We all partake of the one loaf and that is what we celebrate when we come together each Sunday.

Today, the Church celebrates Corpus Christi, the Feast of the Body of Christ. This feast originally dates to the thirteenth century when for many historical reasons, believers went from altar to altar, to gaze at the consecrated host. I suppose many expected favors or answers to prayers by participating in this private devotion. But these believers got so wrapped up in **gazing at** the body of Christ that they stopped **receiving** the body of Christ. So, it was common for most people not to receive communion in those times.

At the beginning of this century there was a renewal in our understanding and frequent reception of communion was encouraged. Then the reforms of the Second Vatican Council invited us not just to look at the body of Christ, but to receive and become the Body of Christ.

Since then, the emphasis has been on participating in the communal celebration of the Eucharist or Mass and on the action of becoming food for others. In other words, we are called to be the Body of Christ to others both inside and outside this community. So how do we accomplish this?

I believe that to be the Body of Christ to others we must first be the Body of Christ as a community. We are called to share our gifts with others. Then it is in the sharing of ourselves as the Body of Christ that we become the Body of Christ to others. So, it is not enough to believe, we must believe and then act on our beliefs. It is not enough to come and worship, but we must come, worship and give ourselves to the community like Christ gave himself to us.

Today's reading from the Gospel of John is taken from the sixth chapter and Jesus had just fed a large crowd with 5 loaves and 2 fish. The crowd was so impressed with Jesus and His works they followed Him even across the lake of Galilee. However, Jesus did not want them to believe only because He fed them physically. He begins to tell them that there is a greater hunger in the human condition than physical hunger—it is spiritual hunger. And to that end He said that He himself is the solution. "I am the Bread of Life" he says, "I am the living bread which came down from heaven."

We first must receive the Body of Christ in and through Christ's love for us then we become love to others. We become a sign to the world that we are **believers in action**. We must be willing to come and give whatever we can to others around us. It may be our ability to teach children. It may be our ability to visit the sick or homebound. It may be reaching out to others less fortunate through financial or personal involvement.

Whatever it is, being the Body of Christ is being spiritual bread to others in our actions. But for us to do this, we first must be willing to **receive** the love of God through Christ. We must be willing to let God nurture us in his love. We must acknowledge the awesome gift God has given us when His only Son became one of us and sacrificed Himself for us. Christ gave of Himself. He left nothing behind.

Today, we are called to do the same. To give of our total selves! And this week let us ask ourselves, how can I give of myself more fully to those around me? How can I be the Body of Christ to someone this week? How can I feed someone the nourishment they need?

Whatever our gifts are, time, talent or treasure, we are called to share them as members of the same body. So today, as we come to receive the Body of Christ at communion time, let us acknowledge loudly that we believe by saying "Amen" with some vigor. Then as we go forth from here let us take the task of being the Body of Christ to someone this week in a new way.

"Because the loaf of bread is one, we, though many we are, are one body for we all partake of the one loaf" (1 Cor. 10:17)

Being a Friend to God

In his book, "A Friendship Like No Other," Father William Barry introduces
the whole concept of God as Friend. For many of us, that is a radical new
concept. Actually, it is a really profound way to view our relationship
with God and casts God in a very different light. It is that God is not just
our father, but a friend who cares for us as a friend would care for us.

In Chapter 9, Fr. Barry takes his understanding to a new level. He reflects
on the other part of that relationship, namely, we are being a friend
to God. Wow! That is radical in so many ways. I can understand that
God is our friend or Jesus is our friend, but it is quite different for us
to be God's friend. Imagine when a person whom you love is hurting,
suffering in some way, your heart bleeds for them and you suffer with
them. You can feel their pain. If your spouse or your child is sick with
a debilitating illness, your heart literally goes out to them and you want
to do anything to relieve their suffering—their pain.

Now reflect about God in that same way. Imagine what it would be like for
God to suffer. He illustrated this with a very powerful reflection. It is
a little hard to hear but powerful. Imagine a child who is radically and
seriously abused sexually and how God suffers and is deeply saddened
as that child is suffering at the hands of another child that he created.
Imagine how God is saddened that the freedom he gave this other
person is now being abused by another person. Imagine how God must
be deeply and profoundly saddened in that moment.

As I reflected on that example, my heart was opened. I felt God's pain on
a deeper level understanding that God was suffering while somebody
else suffers, like a parent who is helpless and hurt when their child is
in pain. It was the freedom that God gave one person that is now being
used by one human to abuse another. I realized how painful that must
be for God.

The image of us being God's friend is very helpful to unlock what we have
heard in today's scriptures because today's scripture talks about the law
and going above the law. We are continuing to hear from the Sermon on

the Mount. There is more than just the law, Jesus says. The first reading is referring to the Israelite people. In the second reading, Paul speaks to the Corinthian community, telling them to be focused on imitating Christ. It is beyond Paul or Peter, Apollos or anyone else; it is all about Christ and God. But how do we get there, to focus solely on Christ?

The key is this new aspect of our relationship with God: God as our friend and we being friends with him. When we do this then we are willing to sacrifice for each other. For example, think of marriages and the love people share or think of a deep friendship we have with somebody whom we love —how you are willing to do something for somebody because we love them and not that I *must do it* but that I *want to do it*.

The contract of marriage is a law, right? We say, "I am married to you and I have an obligation under the law." A marriage is a contract between two individuals who promise to love one another till death. If people only lived by the letter of the law of that contract of marriage, we would have a ton more divorces. What brings the marriage alive is the love that exists within the marriage and we go beyond the contract, beyond the letter of the law of marriage; "You are my wife; you are my husband. I love you." It is not in the contract that you make coffee for one another. It is not in the contract that you are going to give me a kiss in the morning and tell me how much you love me. That is not in the contract, but it is sure important for the marriage that we express the love we share.

Yes, love goes beyond the contract and it is the law of love, not the letter of the law but the law of love. When we are in that space, we sacrifice for the other because the other has a need and not because it feels good. That is what we are called to do —to go beyond the law, not just now in our marriage relationships but in all relationships.

For example, we know we are called to spend time in prayer. We should not only spend time in prayer but willingly spend time in prayer because God is our friend and we want to be a friend to God and thus want to spend time with him.

Today, may we find a way to re-assess our relationship with God as not only that God is our friend but that we are friends to God. May we find a way to go above the letter of the law today and move into the law of love in three ways. (1) With somebody with whom we are in a current relationship; someone who is our spouse or child or parent and to go beyond the letter of the law and do something extraordinary that says and communicates how much we love them. (2) With somebody who is in the extended community, someone we know. Let us do some beautiful act of loving them. (3) With a stranger we will meet this week, somebody who we have never met before. They will be surprised by our willingness to do something extraordinary for them; some act of kindness, generosity, or patience. Today, we go above the letter of the law and into the law of love because not only is God our friend, but we are a friend to God.

Bundle of Old Rags

Once upon a time, there was a great and noble king who decided to celebrate the coronation anniversary of his 30th year of reigning over his kingdom. He decided to invite everyone in the kingdom to come to his party that was to be held at the palace banquet hall. The only condition was that everyone was to wear formal attire. So, everyone got ready and there was great excitement in the kingdom.

A young apprentice carpenter, Peter, knew he was not able to go because he did not have any formal attire. On the afternoon of the actual party, Peter went to the palace and stood outside and looked inside wondering what the festivities would be that night. Just then, somebody turns to him and says, "What's up? Why are you so sad young man?" Startled, he turns around and sees that it is the king himself. "Oh your majesty, I'm sorry, I didn't know it was you." He stutters and stumbles over his words as he says, "I cannot go to the reception today because I do not have the fine clothing, the formal clothes that you have required." "No, I'll have none of that," says the King. He calls his son and tells Peter to go with him. "He will give you the clothes that you need; you must come to the reception." So, the Prince gladly brings him into the palace and gives him a beautiful set of clothes telling Peter that these are fine garments, made of fine linen, silk and wool and they will last much longer than those clothes that Peter was wearing. He then asks Peter, "So give me these other clothes and we will throw them away." Peter says, "No. No. No. I may need these clothes. I might need them." But the Prince tells him, "No. If you need them, come to me and I will give you another set of clothes. You will not need them." But Peter insists even more; "No, no, I don't know when I might need these." So, the young Prince says, "Well, okay, the party is about to begin so we must go in." Peter bent down, picked up his bundle of old rags, put them under his arm and went into the reception with the Prince.

For the entire evening, Peter wasn't quite able to enjoy himself because he had this bundle of rags under his arm. He could not dance because he had only one arm free. He could not really eat or drink because he only had one hand; he could only sample the food and sample the drinks. He felt a little out of it, so he stayed on the edge of the dance floor and along the wall for most of the night because he was carrying his bundle of old rags.

All in the kingdom were delighted because they had such a wonderful and generous king. After the reception was over and the party had come to an end, they went away happy having enjoyed a day and evening of festivities. Peter on the other hand went away sad. He was never able to enjoy the reception and wondered why everybody else did not have a bundle of old clothes as well.

This story is very much like life. We have so much in our lives; we have so many good things going on yet so often we will have a bundle of old rags underneath our arm. What is in our "bundle of old rags" that we won't let go of? What is it that we hold onto so much that we cannot enjoy and engage in the festivities of life that God presents to us every day?

Sometimes they are things or possessions. Sometimes they are ideas or concepts. Sometimes they are old hurts and pains. We are so set on holding onto them that we can never really enjoy the gift of life that God has presented to us. It is our choice to do so. We are the ones like Peter in the story, who hold on to this bundle, insisting that we might need that hurt; we might need that concept; we just might need those things, whatever those things are.

In today's Gospel Jesus is very blunt about what He wants us to do. He wants us to focus on Christ alone. He wants us to focus on the message that He is the son of God and to focus all our energy on God and Himself. If we do that first, then all the other things will sort themselves out.

During hard times, there is no question we worry about what we are going to wear, what we will eat and what we will drink. Those are some real concerns and Jesus acknowledges that reality. But if we focus on God first, then the others will take care of themselves. Now it sounds easy, but it is not so easy to do. Over the years, we have somehow collected a "bundle of old rags" of stuff that we treasure and hold onto. Sometimes we forget that we have the bundle, but we cannot dance the dance of life with just one hand. We need both hands to dance the dance of life.

Today, as we come forward to the table and are reminded of the challenge that God is asking us to choose Him first, may we leave that bundle at the table. What is it that we need to put at the foot of this table and be done and say, "I will leave it here today?" Is it the hurts, or pains of the past? Or is it just ideas that we hold on to, ideology that we hold onto that holds fast, holds us on a path of narrowness? Or is it just that we have too much stuff in our lives? Our society tells us time and time again to go after more stuff: the new iPhone, the new Droid, the new computer, the latest car, the bigger home, more clothes, and the list goes on and on.

Today, we have the opportunity to listen once again to Christ, to set Christ as our primary and first goal and then all other things will be sorted out. Today, let us ask ourselves what is in our "bundle of old rags?" And will we leave them here?

Blessing or Curse

One of the things I love to do is finding shortcuts to doing things, especially when it comes to work on the computer. For example, Command X is to cut; Command C is to copy, and Command V is to paste. They are called keystrokes and they make life quicker when using the computer. Actually, there are lots of other shortcuts. There is a whole market behind them called macros and you can actually program your computer to get shortcuts to do all sorts of things. Now I know it seems strange –is it really important to save an extra 2 or 3 seconds, converting 4 or 5 clicks on the mouse into one keystroke? It is not always so much about the time as much as it is about the achievement of being able to do it in a shorter time.

I also do it in neighborhoods when driving. When I am going somewhere, I love to find the shortest route there. I am always looking for a shortcut to a place. It happens in our lives in many other ways. For example, the whole restaurant business has figured out we like shortcuts, so it has fast food restaurants. We go and we pick up our food, we go home and eat it. But they have also realized that sometimes we don't actually like all of it done for us; so they prepare everything for us and these are called frozen meals. Then we have other ones where we want fresh food. We go into a store, get all the different food components, they do everything for us and then we go home and just put it on the grill or whatever. All are shortcuts to doing the work that we are called to do.

It also happens sometimes in careers. People like to take shortcuts trying to take a step here and there to get up the proverbial corporate ladder. It also happens in finances. We do extraordinary things to get ahead in our wealth accumulation. For example, how many of us have not bought a lottery ticket at some point. That too is a short cut! Most of us would like to win the lottery. What that is based on is our hunger and our want to find a shortcut. The reality is that there are all sorts of possible shortcuts in all parts of our lives. But today in the Gospel, Jesus ends the Sermon on the Mount by making it very clear there is no shortcut in discipleship. He says you cannot just say, "Lord, Lord" at the end. It won't cut it, He says. It won't fool me. There is no shortcut. The only way to the Father is through Christ, in being and acting like Christ. Matthew is completely convinced and says it again at the end of his Gospel. He reinforces how we are to act with one another in what it is that counts, not just our words but that our words match what we do. So, it is not "Lord, Lord" that will get us into heaven but "Lord, Lord" and our actions.

In other words, it is the hard work of living out the faith every day by always doing those small tasks of doing the right thing for the right reasons.

As they were going into the Promised Land, Moses set laws before the people and said to them, "I set before you a blessing or a curse; life or death." He tells them, I give you this opportunity to live life to the fullest, live the commandments, every single one of them; he implores them to live the command of the Lord. And so it is for us too. If we do likewise, we will be blessed, and we will have life. But if we do not, then we will be cursed, and we will not have life. Paul reminds us and converts this into –living out the law is not just about living out the law but is living Christ. The center point of our life is always living Christ to others. At times this is very hard. Indeed, there is nobody here who gets it right all the time. What we do then, is come together to recognize that we are not just saved as individuals, we are also saved as a community of disciples. When we falter and fail, we help each other up. We help each other to get back onto the right path and turn our face back to Christ and rebuild our house on Christ. Yes, we all fail. In some way, shape or form we may fail, sometimes in private matters; sometimes in public ways but we are all called to bind together and to help each other. We are called to hold each other accountable to the way of the cross, to the way of Christ Jesus because that is who we are as Christians. We don't just get saved as individual Christians, but we also get saved as a community of believers in Christ Jesus. This is where it becomes very important to us to help each other when we falter, to help each other when we are in pain, to help each other when we are suffering through a loss of someone in our family or in our community. Together we help each other; together we remain strong disciples; together we build our spiritual homes upon the rock of Christ.

Weaving the Divine Thread

Today, like Moses, I set before you a blessing and a curse: a blessing if we choose to obey His commandment in every little way, a blessing if together we help others when they falter and fall, a blessing if we build our homes on Jesus Christ, a curse if we fail to do so.

Water of Forgiveness; Waves of Mercy

Sometime ago, I had the opportunity to visit with a friend at his house in Seascape by Seacliff Beach near Aptos. While out walking on the beautiful sandy beach I realized it was easier to walk along the water's edge where the waves came in instead of the deep loose sand of the beach. While I was walking along there, I stopped, and I glanced back and realized all my footprints had all been washed away by the waves of the ocean as the water receded. Eventually, they completely wiped away my footprints so you would never even know that I had been there.

Every time I think of God's mercy, I think of that image. That no matter what we do or where we have walked, the Lord's waves of mercy come upon wherever we have walked in our life and wipe away all our sins. They literally leave us completely clean once again. It is a very powerful image to think of that no matter what we do, no matter how deep our footprint might go down into the sand of our lives, no matter how deep our sin runs, the Lord's mercy eventually restores us to wholeness again.

Now the irony of this is that unless I turned around, I would never have realized those footprints were restored to natural beauty. So too it is with our lives. Unless we stop and turn around and face the Lord, we do not know that we have been forgiven. In other words, the act of reconciliation requires of us to turn toward God and acknowledge what we have done, to allow the waves of mercy and God's forgiveness to actually take place in our lives.

Forgiveness, mercy and righteousness are the very themes of today's first reading and the Gospel. The image that the prophet Hosea uses is a slightly different metaphor. He uses the image of the morning sun burning off the fog. The fog is our unfaithfulness and the morning dew is the residual of our sinfulness. The morning sun burns brightly upon all the land, burning off all the fog. It is a different image but equally as powerful. That God's forgiveness, God's mercy ever reigns supreme all the time. There is no fog that the sun, the Lord's forgiveness, cannot burn off. There is no morning dew that the Lord's forgiveness cannot melt. There is no footprint in the sand that the Lord's forgiveness cannot fill in.

In today's Gospel, we hear how Jesus tells the disciples or the would-be disciples, the Pharisees, and us that what He wants is mercy, love and forgiveness more than any words or actions of sacrifice. We hear those words today and we are called to allow the Lord to forgive us our sins. I think the hardest part of our lives is to be able to turn back and realize our sinfulness and to acknowledge that God is able to wash it all clean.

This is what we are called to do as Christians - to allow the Lord to forgive us our sins. No matter how deep the sin goes, no matter how deep our footprint goes into the sand of our lives, the Lord will still restore us to wholeness. This is great news for us as individuals and that is why we come to this table to celebrate.

But there is another part to this reconciliation process - we must become the waves of mercy to others. When others around us are sinful then we are the waves of mercy and we become the water of forgiveness; to allow them to restore themselves to fullness. The reality of our lives is that rarely do our sins only affect us as individuals. Rarely are they so personal that they have no other net effect on anyone else except us. That is a rare sin indeed. Most of our sin, even though it is personal sin, influences those who live around us: our families, our friends even our wider community. Then we have even greater social sins that effect countries far beyond us.

We are called to be part of the water of forgiveness washing away each other's sins. So, it is not just the Lord, we also become part of the Lord's work in others' lives; we reach out to those who are hurting, to those who have sinned. We become part of the wave of God's forgiveness. We literally become the water of forgiveness and the wave of God's mercy.

Today as we go forth from here, renewed and refreshed, having known and reflected upon our own sinfulness, our own need for God's forgiveness, may we then also become God's water of forgiveness and God's wave of mercy to others.

Share Our Time and Not Count the Cost

A dad asked his son what he would like for his approaching sixth birthday. Now his son was usually very specific about what he wanted—to the point of being able to tell them the exact aisle and shelf location at Toys R Us where mom and dad will find the toy or game in question. But this time his son's request was a little different. "I'd like a ball to play with for my birthday." "Great," his dad said. "What kind of ball?" "I guess either a football or a soccer ball." "Well, which ball do you want more?"

The boy thought about it for a minute and said, "Well, if you have some time to play ball with me this year, I'd really like a football so we could throw it back and forth. But if you are going to be really busy again this year, maybe you just better get me a soccer ball because I can play soccer with the rest of the kids on the street."

Dad said, "Tell you what. Let me surprise you. How does that sound?" The little boy said, "That would be great, dad. I really love you." But it was dad who was surprised —surprised and touched that his young son was not so much interested in the gift as in the giver.

In today's Gospel, Jesus saw the crowd's needs. "They were troubled and abandoned." He was moved with pity, moved with compassion by their need for religious leadership. "They were like sheep without a shepherd." He recognized this need and tended to them. He named his twelve apostles, those chosen from his disciples to be sent as their leaders. ("Apostle"—means to be sent.) He told them to cure the sick, raise the dead and heal the leprous. He told them they received gifts from him without cost and so they should give without counting the cost. Jesus set the example by giving of his very self.

We, too, are called to look around us and see the needs of those who we live with and those we work with and tend to their needs. We, too, are called to share our gifts and not count the cost. What are our gifts? What can we all share? Considering that story I shared about the dad and his son, I think one of the greatest gifts we are all given is "time." I really believe it is one of our greatest commodities. No matter how rich or how poor, no matter how educated or uneducated no matter how high-paying or low-paying, no matter how young or old, we all receive the same amount of time each day. With every day we all receive the same 24 hours! We may have more or less years, but on a daily basis, nobody gets any extra time. Yet how we use that time daily will determine how we will be known or for what we will be known.

Do we spend time with our families? Do we spend endless hours at work away from them communicating our priority of work over family? Do we spend time with our children? Whether it be playing ball like the dad in the story or watching them dance or sing. Do we spend time with friends sharing that greatest of gifts?

This week maybe we can spread the Gospel by sharing our gift of time. Maybe we can spend a little extra time with our family whoever it may be: our parents, our children or extended family. Maybe we can share some time with our friends acknowledging that they are important to us by giving them our time. Maybe we can spend some time praying, communicating with God how important His gifts to us really are for us. This week we can be apostles of the good news by spending our precious time in serving others, tending to their needs in the same way Jesus did for His disciples. We can share our time and not count the cost!

Who Am I?

One of the most profound theological and philosophical questions we can ask is, "Who am I?" That question has been asked for centuries and has been answered in a multitude of different ways. It is not the question of "what am I" or "what job do I have" or "where do I live" or "what age" or "how young or old." It has to do with something deeper into the core of who we are. And we ask that question, "Who am I?" If we reflect on it for a moment we can quickly realize because we are human beings of a social nature, we will soon be led to the next question, which is, "whose am I?" In other words, who I relate to becomes important in my life. Who are the most important people and relationships in my life? We start to relate to them and that is where we get our identity from.

That is the very subject matter of today's readings. In the Gospel of Matthew we hear today, Jesus asks the question of his disciples and apostles, "Who do people say that I am?" He is trying to get them to answer the question not just in relation to Himself, but also to get an answer in relation to themselves. So, when Simon Peter says, "You are the Christ, the Son of the Living God," he realizes that who he has come to follow is the Christ, the Son of the Living God. Peter is the disciple of Christ and he realizes that the identity of his own self is very much tied to the identity of who Christ is.

Today, we celebrate the feast day of the apostles St. Peter and St. Paul who are considered the two pillars of our church. Peter is the one on whom the church is founded, like a rock, and sort of the orthodoxy of the church; and then we have Paul, who is the evangelist, the preacher who has gone to all parts of the world to preach to the Gentiles and beyond. We have these two necessary parts of our church. Each of them was called in an individual way to follow Christ. Peter was busy fishing when he was called, "Come follow Me." He drops everything and follows Jesus Christ for the rest of his life. Paul, who was an orthodox Jew, was persecuting the Christians and having them killed if they believed in Christ. He had his conversion experience, and was told to come and follow Him. He, too, turned his life over to the Lord Jesus

Christ and came to follow Jesus in every way, in every aspect. Both gave their lives in service to Christ and His mission even to the point of death. Both of their lives were centered on Jesus Christ, the Son of the Living God and they lived everything according to that primary relationship. That is where they got their meaning from; that is who they are. They became Christians, followers of Christ. We too are called to have Christ at the center of our lives, and to follow Christ in the same way as Peter and Paul.

Now that all sounds wonderful and theologically correct and we say: "Yeah. That is good. Yeah. I agree." But what does that mean in our own life? What does it mean to ask the question, "Who am I?" in relation to our Christ? And how does that change what we do? In other words, I think, we are all here because we all call ourselves Christian; we all call ourselves followers of the Christ. But how does that inform our lives? Does that change the way we are in our daily life?

As an example, for instance, if we claim to be a husband and father – that is who we are – then we must ask the following questions. Does my time get spent according to that relationship or do I find myself just giving my left-over time to my family, my left-over time to my spouse? Do I claim that this is the most important relationship in my life and therefore I am going to spend the time commensurate with that primary relationship?

It is the same when we become Christians. If we claim Christ is the center of our lives and we never spend any time with the Lord, then somehow, we are not saying and doing the same thing.

What we are called to do is re-evaluate our relationships, and to make sure that what we say and do is the same thing. If we claim to be Christian, and we do so because we are here, then we need to make sure that it is a primary relationship with which we spend time. We know that it is hard work and that is why we come together on Sundays. But this Sunday celebration cannot be enough if this is our primary relationship. Coming here for one hour of the week cannot be all there is because then it's not a primary relationship. One hour out of 168 hours in the week is not a primary relationship. We must find a way to spend more time with our Lord during the week and we must spend more time being Christ to others. That is how we live it out; that is how we make it primary. We place Christ in the center of our lives and then we relate our relationship with Christ to our spouse, to our children, our friends, all in relationship with Christ. In other words; we become Christo-centric.

As we come to refresh and renew ourselves at this table today, we come to ask that question of who we are. We come to re-evaluate our primary relationships in our lives and how we can center our lives in real and tangible ways on Christ. Fundamentally, the question we must ask ourselves and spend some time in prayer and reflection on is to ask, "Who am I?" And then to ask, "Whose am I?"

I Lost My Hair Not My Faith

It had been just a couple of weeks since her surgery and the chemotherapy sessions had begun. Every morning, she would comb her hair and every morning, she would pull out clumps of her long beautiful hair from her hairbrush. The reality of the chemotherapy and its side effects was hitting her harder and harder each day.

Then one morning she woke up and rubbed her smooth head with few hairs on it and was literally able to count the last strands of hair on her head. Yet strangely enough, she felt a calm and peaceful presence as she recalled this very passage we heard today, "Even the hairs on our head are counted [by Our Father in heaven]." At that moment, she got a calm sense of the presence of Christ. This presence came to her through her family and friends, most especially through her spouse who was caring for her day and night as she battled the aggressive cancer in her body.

She reflected more about it and realized that with or without hair, God knew her through and through; with or without her hair, God was always present to her; with or without her hair, God would always know who she was. She realized that even though she was still afraid, still nervous about the chemotherapy sessions she was about to undergo, still afraid of the results of the scan that she needed to take, she had a calmness of the presence of Christ, through her loved ones, her family and friends.

Those are the words of Kathryn Lay, a young woman struggling and battling cancer in an article she wrote entitled, "I Lost My Hair, Not My Faith." Even though she was in the midst of incredible struggle, in the depths of pain and illness, she was able to see her God, present to her through her loved ones. It is a very powerful reflection on today's Gospel passage and a great starting place for our reflection.

In today's Gospel Jesus warns the disciples along with you and me that the life of discipleship is not necessarily easy. In fact, it would probably be quite a hard life ahead of them because there would certainly be no less suffering and maybe even more suffering for those who are true followers of Christ. He was trying to encourage them, trying to reassure them that God would always be present to them. No matter what would happen; God would always be with them and take care of them. If God knew even when a sparrow fell, He certainly would know them even more; He would literally count the hairs on everyone's head.

It is the same feeling that Jeremiah is speaking of in the first reading today. He is prophesying the demise and decline of Israel because of their unfaithfulness and he was being persecuted because of his prophecy. Yet, he still recognized, in the midst of his persecution, that God was still present to him even in the midst of suffering.

In our own experience, it seems that when something happens to us regarding our health or something happens to a loved one, somehow the priorities of our lives shift, and we suddenly tend to the bare essentials of life. We realize how important God is in our life and how important our loved ones are to us. None of us want to actually go through something like that to realize how close our God is to us; yet somehow, we still need to do that. It is not that God sends us this illness, this pain or any of this suffering, but in the midst of it, through the pain and suffering, God brings us closer to Him. In the midst of that suffering, we are more aware of God's presence. But we don't want to have to do that, we don't want to be sick to see our God. That is why we come to Mass each week. We come here each week so we can realize how God is not only present to us in the midst of illness but also in the midst of goodness, in the midst of the ordinary things of daily life which we try to tend to here and now. We go to the presence of Christ in our life and realize how blessed we are; how incredibly blessed we are that God is always present to us, caring for us and loving us wherever we are.

There is more than just coming here and realizing this presence in some sort of self-indulgent realization of God. We are called to also go forth from here to be the presence of Christ to others; we are the ones who are called to tend to our sick neighbor; we are the ones who are called like those people in the woman's story today, we are called to be that living presence of Christ to those who are hurting and those who are ill. It is not just simply being in the presence here; it is about taking the presence we receive here and being that presence in other people's lives. As St. Theresa of Avila says so eloquently, "Christ has no hands in this world but yours and mine. Christ has no feet in this world but yours and mine. Christ has no heart in this world but yours and mine," and so we are called to love one another as Christ has loved us.

Today, we may be one of those ill people who is suffering with some illness or disease and are receiving the care and love of others. May we be thankful and grateful for the presence of Christ through our loved ones. And if we are one of the ones who is healthy, then let us know we are called to be the hands, feet and heart of Christ. We are called to reach out today to the people in our lives, in a word of kindness, a word of forgiveness, in an action of generosity, in an action of forgiveness. Today, you and I are the hands, the feet and the heart of Christ. Today, we celebrate the living presence of Christ among us.

Year-Round Christian

About a week ago I was talking with a swim instructor who had just attended a swim meet. She said that it was so obvious which swimmers were year-round swimmers. The ones who had made the sport part of their everyday routine were noticeably faster and stronger. The kids who were only swimming on the team for the summer were just not the same caliber of swimmer. How could they be! They were out of practice since last summer.

I think the same can be said of our faith! If someone was watching us for a day, would they say, "That's a year-round Christian," or would they say that we are just seasonal?

In today's Gospel we hear Jesus invite us to make Him a #1 priority in our lives. We are called to lay down everything and follow Him. To leave it all behind and follow Him to the end! I fully realize that this is truly a tall order! However, don't you think it's strange how we can train so hard for sports but when it comes to living the Gospel, we let it slide?

For example, I remember when I was in college, I played rugby very seriously to play at a national level. I would train for hours every day. Practice for fitness. Practice for skill. Practice for stamina. Practice, practice, practice.

Many of you play baseball, basketball, football or other sports. You know what it is like to put time into practice. We train so that we can excel at our sport and be ready for that moment. Can you imagine if we put that much effort into our faith! Imagine spending hours praying and practicing our faith every day. In one sense that is what Jesus is asking of us. We are called to make discipleship a #1 priority every day.

Today's scripture also gives us an example of how to make that priority. Both in the Gospel and the first reading we are called to be hospitable. In the first reading Gehazi offered room and board to the prophet Elisha. In the Gospel, Jesus asks us to welcome the prophet in his name. So, one of the ways to practice our faith is to offer hospitality. This does not necessarily mean that we need to open our doors to every stranger. Maybe some of you students present here tonight can open your circle of friends to an outsider, to someone at school who always seems to be friendless. Or maybe for those who work, we can open our circle of friends to those of our co-workers who are always left out of conversations. Or maybe for those who are retired or at home we can extend a warm greeting to old and new neighbors and open our hearts to new friendships.

This week we can be "year-round Christians" by opening our hearts to those who seek love and friendship. Today we can practice, practice, and practice our faith. This week by being hospitable we can practice our faith and be year-round Christians!

My Yoke is Easy!

There is a story told of a young boy who wanted a dog. His parents brought him to the dog breeder to let him choose the puppy for himself. When they arrived, the owner told them the puppies cost between $200-$300 each. The boy's face dropped for he only had $50. However, the owner whistled, and all the little puppies came running to the boy. At the very back was a little crippled dog trying hard to run but unable to keep up with the rest. The boy's eyes lit up with delight and he shouted, "I want that little lame dog back there." But the owner protested saying that the little puppy was of no use to anyone. He would not be able to play ball with the boy, nor would he be able to run after him. But the boy persisted even more!

The owner tried again, saying that in conscience he could not charge for such a dog. Indeed, if he wanted the dog, he could have him for free! The boy said, "No!" He would pay the same price as the other dogs. He would give him $50 now and pay $20 a month until he paid in full for the dog. Reluctantly, the owner agreed.Taking the little lame puppy, the boy rolled up his pants leg and showed the owner his artificial leg. The boy said that indeed the dog would not run after him because he cannot run. Nor will the dog play ball with him because he cannot play ball. But the dog will be his friend because they know each other's pain!

We mostly identify with people who suffer or who are in pain if we, ourselves, have suffered a similar pain. For example, if someone loses a parent to death, we can identify with their loss if we have already lost our own parent. We also can extrapolate our experiences to help us relate to those who suffer. This is called empathy—to personally experience someone's emotions. Not sympathy or pity towards to others, but a genuine empathy, to feel pain with someone.

God understands our pain and is always there for us. In order that we know that God really is there for us, He became one of us in Jesus. Jesus walked in our shoes. He knows our pain as one of us. He really understands us even to the point of death! He could have prevented all of that since He was God, but He chose not to so that we could understand that He knows our pain. In doing so He shows us genuine empathy!

Today's Gospel tells us how the Father and Jesus are one and how if we know Jesus then we will know the Father. Jesus also offers to share our burdens. Notice that He does not promise to take our pain away! Rather He promises to share the load with us. He invites us to take his yoke and make our burden lighter. We are called to bind ourselves to Jesus and allow Him to share our load.

It is important to understand "yoke" in agricultural terms. In farming communities of old, two oxen were bound together using a yoke, a wooden bar tied over their shoulders. This enabled them to share the workload. Notice that work in the field to be plowed was not reduced. Rather, the workload was shared between two oxen making the job easier.

In a similar manner Jesus invites us to share our burdens with Him. If we bind ourselves to His yoke, then we will find that our burden is made lighter. We are called to bind ourselves to the Lord and live in His Spirit as Paul said. We do this by sharing our problems and burdens with one another. We have an old Irish adage I love, "A joy shared is twice the joy, a sorrow shared is half the sorrow." Who in our life needs to share a sorrow or a joy? And in so doing we lighten their burden and make their yoke easy!

Letter from God

Recently, I had the opportunity to attend the Broadway musical "Billy Elliott."
It was a story about Billy Elliott, a young boy who wanted to become a
dancer. But he was from a coal mining town in Northern England. This
was in 1984 during the strikes between the coal miners and Margaret
Thatcher and her government who were determined to break the backs of
the coal mining unions. One needs to understand that the scene is set in
a town where there are 300 years of generations of people who worked in
the coal mines. Consequently, the expectation was that every man became
a coal miner: grandfather, father, son, and grandson. In this particular
situation, the father was a coal miner and the son was a coal miner but the
young boy was too young, so he was learning to be a boxer. While he is
taking boxing lessons, he discovers dancing. He sees that there is a ballet
class that follows his boxing class and he finds that he loves to dance.

During all this, there is a very powerful part where he is trying to discover
the dancer within himself. The dance instructor asks him to bring
different things that might describe who he is or what he cherishes. He
brings all these miscellaneous things that are irrelevant and then he
pulls out of his pocket a letter from his mother who died while Billy
was still very young. She had asked him not to open the letter until he
was 18 years old, but he opened it at age 12, and he said, "It's probably
a good thing I do it now." The letter is powerful:

"Dear Billy,
  I must seem a distant memory
  Which is probably a good thing
  And it will have been a long, long time
  And I will have missed you growing
  And I'll have missed you crying
  And I'll have missed you laugh

  Missed your stamping and your shouting
  I have missed telling you off
  But please, Billy, know that I was always there
  I was with you through everything

And please, Billy, know that I will always be
Proud to have known you
Proud that you were mine
Proud in everything
And you must promise me this, Billy
In everthing you do
Always be yourself, Billy
And you always will be true
Love you forever
Love you forever.
Ma"

It was a powerful point in the musical because Billy was struggling with breaking away from the expectations of being a coal miner. Before Billy's mother died, she gave her son a letter so that he would read it when he grew up.

The Lord God does something different to us. He writes his word and puts it in our soul, but He does not ask us to wait until we are 18 years old to read it; He wants us to read it right away, to come to know Him. Just like Billy Elliott's mother, God is with us through it all, no matter what. But when we do not allow God in, we miss out on that relationship.

Today's scripture tells us the word of God is like a seed planted and our hearts are the soil in which the seed is planted. It is a very powerful illustration of how we are called to be a fruitful soil ready for the word of God. The seed is already planted in our soul when God created us. We must discover who is it that God asks us to be. God has something planned for each one of us, something magnificent, something great. We are called to bring that to life and to truly expose it, to let the seed grow in our lives and then to bear fruit so that others can lay witness to our Christian life.

Maybe it sounds so wonderful, so easy but it's hard to do. Like the Gospel says, there are worldly anxieties and distractions and there is the evil one who will tempt us to do otherwise. The question is how to make sure that the word has a place to grow. One way is to come here to the table to nourish and to till the soil of our hearts so that the seed has somewhere to grow. Another is through the actions and words that we do outside of here. Every little thing that we do that is kind and generous is a way in which we can bring that word to life.

There is one powerful way we can do it for each other and will help things grow in our lives, in the gardens of our lives, in the gardens of our hearts. What if we did something like what Billy Elliott's Mum did for him, that is to write a note to our child and say something that can be memorable, something that would be powerful, something from our heart that is more than just the casual word, something that would be momentous.

I know that the written word seems old fashioned and we don't hand write notes very much anymore but I really believe it is powerful to write a note to your son or daughter or to your mother or father and say how much they mean to you. Let us not wait until the time is too late to write that note; may we not wait till they are eighteen. It is important that we let each other know how important they are now because the road can get difficult and it can get very dark on that road. Sometimes we need to be able to open letters to remind ourselves of the people we journey with, who are good and who love us.

Today, we come to be encouraged that we are God's children and His word is already in our hearts and we want to enable that to grow with what we do in our prayer and in our actions. Let us also foster that growth in other people. Maybe writing a memo or a letter or note to somebody we love this day will touch their soul and may become the fruitful soil where the seed of God's word may grow in their heart.

Google Effect

How many of you remember the slide rule? Some of you don't even know what I am talking about. A slide rule was a ruler that had a sliding section in the center, and it was the quickest way to multiply, divide or square-root, etc. It pre-dated the electronic calculator. One could even do trigonometry and calculus with it. My graduating high-school class was one of the first classes to not use the slide rule.

I remember there was an enormous controversy among the educators when I was graduating. They were saying that the students who did not learn the slide rule would be at a significant disadvantage because we would rely on a calculator. Some feared we would never know how to do math properly again. The controversy went on for years.

I don't know if you read recently in the newspaper an article called the "Google Effect." The Google Effect says that kids today do not retain a lot of the facts that we all learned when we were in school. The reason is because they just Google the data! They don't have to waste any brainpower saving data when they can go to Google and find what they need to know. The point is that the exact same controversy is going on today as it was in my day. The young people will lose the essentials and they will be lost as a result of that.

Now, I must be honest with you, I do not believe that any of my older brothers who used the slide rule are any smarter than me because I did not use it. The point being is that the brain has an insatiable appetite to learn and if it does not learn one thing here, it will move over and start learning something else over there. The mind will continue to learn no matter what. Instead of learning how to use the slide rule, we learn how to use the very complicated calculator. And we go from there and learn how to use other things. The same is true when talking about God. The danger is that we sometimes talk about God in black and white images. I call them facts or factoids about God, something we would look up on Google to get an answer. Well, God is beyond those words; God is beyond any single set of words that makes up sentences or paragraphs. The mystery of God is way beyond any of those words and that is one of the reasons why Jesus in today's Gospel speaks in parables. The reason is because parables have a depth of reality to them. They are not factoids; they are not facts and data about God.

A parable is a metaphor or a simile that draws comparisons between God and nature, drawing the mind into a deeper reflection of the mystery of God. It is a metaphor that draws us into thinking more about God, engaging the whole mind and understanding of how God is operating in our lives. As a result, when we listen to the parables, each of us could hear it somewhat differently and we could apply it somewhat differently. Each generation and each community of churches all around the diocese will hear and apply it somewhat differently because the depth of God's love can never be fully comprehended. We come away with some new insights every time we hear them but not the totality of what the parable or what the mystery of God is.

The disciples also struggled with why Jesus spoke to them in parables. Why couldn't He just speak plainly to us so that we could understand? His defense was always that the mystery of God is beyond words. We approach that mystery through parables because it is something that our mind must dive into to open our minds with wonder and awe. Every day is a new day. Every day is a new dawn, a new opportunity to learn something new about life. Our mind wants to know new things; our mind desperately wants to experience the vast immensity of God. Here is the wonderful and exciting thing about life –every day we wake up we can learn something new about ourselves, about other people and about God. Every single day, no matter how long we live, we can discover something new. That's what makes life so incredibly exciting and precious. No day is dull, and every day is an opportunity to open with freshness. We must approach each day with that sense of wonder and awe.

Today's Gospel and parables are speaking about patience of faith. We are called to understand that when we plant the seed, we will not have immediate results. A tree takes time to grow; we must let it grow like the weeds among the wheat. We must let it grow and bear fruit. When we put yeast in the bread, it may take time to leaven the bread, but it does leaven the bread; there is goodness in the midst of all that. So too, we must go back every day to the Lord and allow Him to bear fruit within us. We go back to Him with open eyes and wonder and are prepared to look at life again. Because each day brings us a new dawn, a new day and a new opportunity to learn who God is, who others are and who we are.

The reason we come to the table every Sunday is to celebrate that newness, that freshness together; to receive strength to go out and live it every day.

I know life can deal some serious blows to us. But no matter what happens to us in our life, regardless of physical illness, mental or emotional struggles we can always wake up each day with a new attitude. We know that this day, we can learn something new: new about ourselves, new about others and new about the mystery of God.

The Sun Shines in Our Windows

There is a story told of a young boy who lived in a house on a hill that overlooked a beautiful valley. He would sit out on his porch and look out onto the beautiful valley below and at the gorgeous mountain across the valley. He would marvel at the beauty of God's creation, but, when the sun would set, he would see this beautiful house that sat opposite in the hills, nestled in the trees. When the sun would set, it would shine off the glass in the windows of this house like gold and glisten. It seemed to just sit there like a ball of gold. He marveled at how precious it would be to live in that marvelous house.

One day, he decided he would go visit the house. He packed up a lunch, took a canister of water and trekked out down into the valley and up over onto the other side of the hill. It took longer than he anticipated, and he arrived just before the sun had set. As he looked around, he was rather disappointed to find out that this magnificent house was nothing more than a little cottage nestled in the woods.

When he arrived, the family was very gracious and nice; they welcomed him in, and they gave him a meal. Because it was too late for him to make the trek back, they encouraged him to stay and put out a bed for him in the kitchen. As he was dining and sitting there, one of the girls who lived in the house, about his same age, started to talk to him about how beautiful the valley is. She told him that he would have to wait until sunrise because across the valley, she described, there is this beautiful house that lights up in the morning. And sure enough, he wakes up with great enthusiasm and looks out across the hills and sees this house that dazzles with the rising sun. He was shocked to find out it was his own little cottage.

Today's reading talks about how we can search for a pearl of great price and how we can sell all to find it. What the Lord is telling us is that the Kingdom of God is at hand; that is the message of St. Matthew and his Gospel. We have a temptation to always look across the proverbial valley of our lives and to see other people's homes, other people's lives glistening like gold and we wonder how wonderful it would be to be

116

them, who have God shining on their lives. How wonderful it would be to see our windows glistening like other people's windows seem to glisten. We sometimes forget how blessed that we ourselves are. I think that we forget how great God has already been to us.

The kingdom of God that is referred to in this Gospel passage is already here. The kingdom of God is already here and now; it is here with us. This word of God that we have received and the gift of the Holy Spirit that we have received is the gift we already have. We need to live that out and work it out with great joy in our hearts.

Sometimes, we get distracted. We think that we are not gifted. Instead, we need to adopt an attitude of gratitude for the gifts that we already have. Sometimes we forget to tend to the gifts we have, and we want other gifts. In today's first reading, we have this wonderful section about Solomon. Solomon is asking for wisdom and he asks God to give him an understanding heart so he can be a wise leader of his people. The Lord blesses him and gives him this incredible gift of wisdom because he was so magnanimous in asking for it and nothing for himself. But here is the part that we may have forgotten; Solomon had two sides to him, like a Jekyll and Hyde. Even though Solomon killed several people to be the king, God gave him a guiding heart. Unfortunately, he quickly forgets to attend to that gift. He becomes completely self-absorbed as a king. He had 600 wives, 300 concubines, hardly the ideal for a king, but this is the same Solomon we hear about today. Why? Because he forgot to tend to the gift he was given; he forgot to really listen to the Lord in his own heart. I think that is the danger for you and me. We have a danger of not tending to the gifts that God has given to us.

We are all here today and we all have gifts; we have the gift of health, the gift of family, and the gift of a clear mind. Now, maybe not everything is going well for us. I am not suggesting that all things are easy because they are not. Life sometimes takes us on difficult turns, throws us some serious curve balls, but as the second reading from Paul to the Romans says, all things turn out for the good to those who love God, who believe in God. So, we must take the stance of faith. No matter what happens in our lives, good or bad, God will make good on all things. We choose to believe that and will walk with that faith knowing that God will make good on all.

You see, that is wisdom. That is true wisdom. Those are the words of Christ
Himself. That is what we are called to be as people of faith. Today as
we gather around this table to celebrate with this attitude of gratitude
for what we have been given: family, friends, the gift of life itself, the
gift of education, the gift of so many things that we have in our lives,
may we not look across the proverbial valley of our lives and look into
the houses or windows of other people's homes and see how blessed
they are, but instead realize the sun rises and shines on our home, the
home of our soul where Christ dwells within.

Climbing the Mountain of the Lord

As many of you know I like to hike, and I was recently hiking in Utah and
Colorado. What I would like to do in Colorado is try to climb all the 58
peaks over 14,000 feet and my goal is to celebrate Mass on top of all
those peaks. So far, I have climbed 22 peaks and slowly working my
way through them. These climbs take some serious effort and time. It
can take from 3.5 hours to 6 hours to get to the top. One of the peaks
climbs from 3,500 to 6,500 feet shift in elevation. Towards the top,
the air is very thin, and it takes a great deal of effort, especially those
last 1,000 feet of climbing. From 13,000 to 14,000 feet the air is very
thin, and one moves only a couple of steps at a time before stopping to
breathe. When you get to the top, it is a great joy and gift to be there;
there is *nothing* above you and you are literally on top of the world.
Typically, there is nobody else around and so it is a great sense of
accomplishment. During the midweek there may be two or three other
people hiking that same mountain and, on a weekend, maybe a dozen
on the popular mountains. So, when you get up there, the mountaintop
is yours and it is great.

Last Tuesday my friend and I hiked to the top of Mt. Evans. It was one
of the shorter hikes and it took us only about 3 hours to get to the top.
When we got to the top, you can imagine how disturbed I was to see
the entire mountaintop covered with people. I looked around and said,
"What is going here!" Then I looked below and there was a road; they
all had driven up! We are panting and puffing, and these people just
walked about 100 feet to the top. They were milling around taking
pictures of being at the top of Mount Evans, 14,280 feet. As I sat there
catching my breath, all these thoughts went through my mind. One
thought I had was everyone who came up from the parking lot ought
to carry a 50-pound stone up and down; if they can carry it then they
can take the picture! But as I caught my breath and started to eat a little
lunch, I realized what a gift it was for me to be able to hike at all. A lot of
these people were elderly people who would not have been able to take
any of those steps at all. But the view from up there is so spectacular;
it was such a joy to have other people to share in it even if they had to

walk only 100 feet from the parking lot, just so they could enjoy, just for that moment, what it was like to see the beauty of the mountain from the top. I realized that we had the better part because we had been able to walk and enjoy it for nearly four hours, appreciating every aspect of the mountain until we got to the very top. It is a different perspective when one has hiked it for oneself and I believe our experience is the better part. In today's Gospel, and all of today's readings, we hear how salvation is for everyone. Sometimes when somebody comes late to the faith, we who have been Christians all our lives and have been working hard on living this out, walking up the mountain with the Lord, may think, "Gosh, that's just not really fair. You've been off doing your thing for the last 20 years and now you just kind of get in before the last moment." Sometimes we are envious and other times we refuse to give them full access to the Lord because we feel that they have not worked as hard as we have in our life at being good. Still other times we become jealous because their faith seems to be a little more zealous, they seem to have a little more energy because they have not climbed up the mountain like us. We're a little exhausted, especially close to the end. We believe that others need to do a little bit more to be a good Catholic or to be a good Christian —they must do more than come in at the last moment.

Sometimes we do that even culturally; we think the same thing about people who have a faith that is a slightly different variation from ours or have a different expression from ours. We tend to be a little selfish or stingy with what Jesus offers. We tend to withhold the grace and salvation that God offers to all. The mountain is for everyone, not just for those who can climb. So also, is the Gospel. The Gospel is for everyone. Everyone has been offered grace and everyone is given the opportunity to take that mountain. We ought to take time to realize how gifted we are that we have had the grace to be able to walk the mountain of the Lord knowing that the Lord has been with us all the time. That we have had the better part because we have known the Lord all these years and we have walked with the Lord.

It has been hard work, but it has been good work. It has been the work of the Lord. That is what makes it good. We work it out; we give of our money; we give of our time and we give of our talent. Others have not done that, but we have the better half because we have known the Lord all these years. What a grace that is to be able to walk on the mountain of the Lord knowing that we have enjoyed it all our life. That is a grace and a gift for all of us.

Together we enjoy the grace God offers to all of us, salvation to all through one.

Today, we come to the table, knowing that all are welcome at the table and some of us have been working hard on this mountain, we have the better part.

Twenty-First Sunday of Ordinary Time
Isaiah 22:19-23; Psalm 138; Romans 11:33-36; Matthew 16:13-20

I Know Who I Am

Every day, Tim would go to the care home and visit with her. Each time she would ask Tim who he was and why he was visiting her. And each time Tim would explain who he was and why he was visiting. He would tell the story of all his children and grandchildren, all the activities and all the news of his family. And while he was feeding her lunch each day, he would gently remind her that he was married for 52 years to the same woman and that woman was her. Then each time, she would smile brightly as if told for the first time. That woman was Margaret and Margaret suffers from Alzheimer's. She goes in and out of consciousness.

Tim tends to her every day. Before he leaves, he caresses her gently, kisses her and tells her that he loves her dearly. He knows full well that tomorrow he will have to repeat the whole routine over and over again.

His friends plead with Tim and ask why he continues to put himself through this. They tell him, "She does not even know who you are any more." He would always respond the same way, "But I know who I am."

The reality of our own lives is that we are known by our actions. How we treat one another is how we first know who we are for ourselves and that is how others come to know us. Then they will also listen to us and measure our actions against our words. And we, ourselves, ought to do the same thing for we will be held accountable for what we do and what we say. But when it comes down to it, we will always be judged on how we act and not on how we say we will act. It is our actions that we will be known for.

That is what Jesus asks today, "Who do people say that I am?" He knew who He had been with the people; He had been healing them. He had been forgiving them. He had been preaching to them. But He wanted to know if they knew who He was, not because He didn't know who He was, but He wanted to know if the people could recognize in His actions that He was truly the Son of God.

Many of the spectators had it wrong. But Peter, His closest friend, knew who He was. Peter said, "You are the Christ, the Son of the living God."

Because Peter knew Him the best, he had spent the most time with Him, he of all people would have known. But it was not just because of that, but because as the reading today says, because the heavenly Father revealed this to Peter. In our own lives, our closest family and friends know us the best; and that is not always convenient because they know us best in the good and the bad ways. We cannot really hide anything from them. We might try to hide the odd bad thing, an odd bad habit, an odd bad phraseology we might use, if you would. The reality is our spouses, our children and our parents know us well. I mean, who among us as parents, has not had their child say something to you, pointing out the inconsistency in the words we use and the actions we have done. And they remind us, "But that is not what you said Daddy; that is not what you said Mum." Or "That is not what you did Mum; you did this." And we go, "Oops." The reality is they watch everything. They listen to it and they mimic it. It is true also of those who are otherwise close to us. They know us through and through and we must be honest with ourselves. Who are we?

Yes, as human beings, we are people with limitations, human limitations and human weaknesses. But we are also people with incredible potential, an unbelievable potential to care for and love others. Above all of that, we are Christians; that is who we claim to be. As Christians we claim not to play to our weakness but to play to our strength, to be the best we can be, the kindest we can be, to be the most loving, the most forgiving, the most willing to serve others. That is who we claim to be with our words. But do our actions lay claim to that same creed; that we are Christians in what we say and in what we do?

We must reflect on that. We must be honest with ourselves in "Who do people say that I am." It starts with the question, "Who am I?" Am I really living up to those difficult words of discipleship, to love others, to forgive others and to serve others? These are not easy things to do, but that is our claim.

In Tim loving his wife Margaret, he continues to love her not because she knows who he is but because he knows who he is; he is her husband of 52 years. You and I have responsibilities as members of the body of Christ, to love others, to forgive others, to serve others and it starts with a question that we must first ask ourselves, "Who am I" and "Who do people say that I am?"

Simplexity: Every Action Counts

There is a new field of study called "simplexity." It maintains that all major phenomena such as all major world events, traffic and even politics contain a series of events that take place which can all be traced back to a trigger event which is a simple incident. It states that if that simple incident had not happened, then all the other things would not have happened. It is called "simplexity theory." It maintains that all human history is determined by such events. For example, the Watergate scandal happened because a security guard spotted a piece of tape on the door latch so that it wouldn't lock. As a result, he knew that someone had burglarized the office. That was the trigger event that spawned the investigation. It was the event that triggered everything and without that, they would never have found out.

The powerful components or concepts in this theory are called "choke points." Consider them, if you would, to be like a junction box; it could go one way or the other, depending on what comes thru this small event. They are like keyholes into the complexity of life events on life's journey. For instance, in 1854, there was a massive outbreak of cholera in London. It could have killed hundreds of thousands of people. The disease was traced back by a physician, Dr. John Snow, who found that this outbreak occurred from a contaminated watering station. It was the water pump that was causing the problem. So, he simply turned off the water pump and the cholera outbreak stopped in its tracks. Now if he had not turned off the pump, for sure, thousands more people would have died. All that was needed was a simple turning off the pump.

These "choke points" happen in any series of events and most major events that happen in our world can happen in this way. The theory says that basically all complex events come down to a simple series of events.

In our own lives, we often wonder, "If I had not met so and so on such and such a date, I would not have met my wife or my husband and then where would I be"; "If I had not said that comment on that particular day, such and such thing may not have happened." Then there is a trigger of events. Today we hear in scripture of one such choke point in human history.

Christ had to die to be risen from the dead. Right? In dying, the crucifixion was part of this series of simple events that produced the greatest event that ever happened in human history. But today we hear in the Gospel, Peter is trying to stop it. Unbeknown to himself, he is trying to force the "choke point", the junction box, to go a different way. As a result, Jesus rebukes him quite harshly. He says, "Get behind me Satan, you don't know what you are doing; you are thinking as human beings do, not as God does."

We believe as Christians that every one of our actions has the potential to be that junction box. We believe that every one of our words and every one of our thoughts can trigger a series of positive events or negative events, depending on what or how we act at that moment. That may seem like a burden to have but that is what we believe as Christians. That is why we spend time thinking about and reflecting on how our actions are oriented towards our God. Are they oriented in such a way as to help us to be better people, or to be better organized in our own way of life? This weekend we celebrate Labor Day and we recognize the importance of labor, of work in our life. Catholic social teaching teaches us that work is not just a privilege, but it is a right. It is something that we ought to do and we ought to do it well. There are also choke points along the way. How we treat people at work has an impact on others and how they treat others. So, we have what is called the dignity of the workplace and we recognize that today and realize how important it is for us to become aware of the workplace and those who are working.

For example, many of us have gone on vacation these last few months and stayed in a hotel or a motel somewhere. Let us ask ourselves how we treated the lowest employee that we came across. From the people who cleaned our rooms, to the janitors in the hallway or the restaurant staff, did we acknowledge them or pretend they did not even exist? There is an opportunity here for us to make a change, to be a junction box and change their day. We have the opportunity to see each one of those as choke points in our day.

Another choke point is in the environment in which people work. People have the right to a good working environment which sets off a choke point in the right way. We have the potential to enable our work environment or somebody else's work environment to be a positive experience or a negative one. My point is that each one of us is going to be presented today with opportunities that may be choke points in our day. How will we decide? We may never know how these choke points affected others. But we believe as people of the Gospel that every single one of our actions makes a difference; every single one of our decisions; every single one of our thoughts and words have an impact on others. They are, if you would, the choke points in our daily lives.

Today, we celebrate at our Lord's Table, the gift of the greatest choke point in all of history, the death and resurrection of Christ Jesus. We recognize that we will be given opportunities and it is up to us to make choices as followers of Christ to do the will of the Father.

Good Friends Challenge!

When we are born into this world as a child, we are completely dependent on others for our wellbeing. At first, we depend on our mothers for our food then we depend on our family, whether it be our mother or father, grandmother and grandfather, or other siblings. We depend on them for our physical needs, our emotional, mental and even spiritual needs. Later in life we try to do more for ourselves and assert our independence from our parents. Those are often called our rebellious years—teenage years!! But if we are honest with ourselves, we can never be fully independent. We need others to be in relationship with. We need friends to love us and us to love them. We need each other! We are not made to be alone!

The movie Shrek is about an ogre who lives alone in a swamp until one day he is invaded by characters from every fairytale. Unhappy about losing his swamp he makes a deal with the king to rescue the princess for him and then he'll have his swamp back. So he goes off with his new friend, the donkey, to rescue the Princess Fiona. They do rescue the princess and return to the king. On the way back, he had a big falling out with his friend, the donkey and his new love Fiona. They all part their separate ways and Shrek returns to his swamp all alone. However, after returning to the swamp he is lonely now. At one point, the donkey comes to take his share of the swamp and Shrek argues with him. They get into a big argument and the donkey tells him the truth about Shrek acting mean and nasty to him and Princess Fiona. Shrek asks if that is the case then why are they still here? Donkey reminds him that he cares for him and forgives him and that is what friends do—forgive one another! Shrek is not convinced until he hears that he misunderstood what Fiona had said. Then in a humble moment asks donkey to forgive him. They become friends again!

Notice what happens here: Donkey goes to his friend Shrek and challenges him with the truth. He tells him alone that his behavior was not appropriate. He tells him to get his act together. He cares enough for him to challenge him and in doing so, risks their entire friendship. Good friends challenge each other to grow and we are dependent on others for that growth. In today's scripture we hear about how to deal with one another. We hear from Jesus about how to be friends. Why do you suppose that Jesus is telling us how to be friends? Maybe it is because we love our friends or at least care for them and He wants us to know how to love one another. He understands it is our closest friends with whom we will have the greatest friction and so He suggests a method to deal with disagreement. He says that we must first go to the person we have the disagreement with and give them the opportunity to hear from us alone. Not to go to someone else but the offender in person. We are told to go to them but not to assert our need to be right but instead to go to them out of love and care for them. We go to them so they can learn and grow themselves. If they do not listen to us, we bring someone else to witness. If that does not work, go to the Church. If that does not work, then we treat them like a Gentile. In this country I guess that must mean suing them!!

It seems to me that when someone comes to us to correct us, we can often get very defensive! "No! You misunderstand what I said!" "No! That is not what I meant!" "That is not what happened!" We can become so defensive that it is next to impossible to approach us. I think we need to allow others to correct us. I also think we need to be very gentle and caring in correcting others recognizing they are fragile and in need of understanding. And I believe we need to be explicit about giving that permission, explicit in our actions and in our willingness to listen to correction.

Is there someone in our life we can give permission to challenge us? Is there someone in our life that we need to challenge? This week we can be a good friend to others by allowing them to challenge us with the truth because the truth comes from God. We can also be a good friend by challenging them gently and kindly when they need it. Today, do we care enough to listen to correction, and do we give it when we need to?

Forgive. How Many Times?

"If my brother sins against me, how many times should I forgive? As many as seven times?" Peter asked. He must have felt rather accomplished in asking it because the tradition up until that point only required the Jews to forgive three times. Indeed, more dominant in the Jewish scriptures is the passage, "an eye for an eye and a tooth for a tooth." Jesus tells Peter something radical. He doesn't say, "Yes; it's seven times." He says, "seventy-seven times" which was an expression basically saying every time!

Is it *every* time we are called to forgive? Is it possible the Lord is asking us to forgive that one person who hurt us deeply? That spouse who wreaked our lives in a bitter divorce. That ex-boyfriend or girlfriend who lied about our relationship? That sibling who remains completely self-centered and destroys every family gathering with their antics? That ex-friend who betrayed us so many years ago? Is the Lord serious that we must forgive *every* time? It is hard to conceive of such a generous and big heart to forgive. How much harder it would be to forgive those who caused such grievous offenses such as rape or incest. How could the Lord ask such a thing? How much harder it would be to forgive those who perpetrated the events of 9/11? They created havoc in our country and world. Are we still called to forgive? Not only did we lose 3,000 people that day but also how many more lives were wrecked because of those events. Many of those involved who were in the Towers and the many first responders were wounded and seriously maimed because of it, leaving their families devastated. Are we really called to forgive all that? And the answer is yes. Everyone. Wow! That's so hard to hear.

It may be possible for those of us who were not directly involved in those events but as a nation it is hard to forgive such atrocities. It is hard to allow this to come into our land, come into our hearts and then to just simply forgive them. It is just as hard to forgive somebody who has grievously offended us, who has hurt us personally. Yet, the Lord says to every one of us, "Forgive every time."

How providential it is that these readings fall on this day, the anniversary of 9/11. These words are meant for all of us, not just those affected by this event but also those involved in everyday offenses who offend us and who hurt us. We are called to forgive every time. Jesus goes one step further and tells us the condition which we are to forgive. We are to forgive "from the heart." Jesus is asking so much of us!

In the ancient time, the heart would have meant not the emotional heart or the place where we have feelings; instead, it would have meant the place of the intellect. In other words, forgiveness is a choice of the will. We can choose to forgive. We can choose to not be determined by the events of the past but choose the freedom in forgiveness and to always remain free. That is what Christ wants for us. He gave us freedom by His death on the cross and He wants us to remain free. We know that if we do not forgive then we lock ourselves up in our own prison, we become captives ourselves in our own prison of hatred and unforgiveness. By forgiving, we set ourselves free to live once again.

Any of us who has ever had a grudge or a pain so deep that we are unwilling to forgive knows what it means to be in that prison cell of our own mind of unforgiveness. Yet, we are called again to forgive. How do we do this? How can we possibly forgive those horrendous acts? How can we forgive those acts that happened to us?

Let me read to you a few words that were written by a child, a child who was about to be gassed in the chamber of a Nazi concentration camp. He wrote on a piece of paper and stuck it in his pocket knowing that his captors, torturers and murderers would find it. This was the prayer that he wrote. "Oh Lord remember not only those of good will but also remember those of ill will. But, do not remember all the suffering that they have inflicted upon us instead remember all the fruits that have been born because of this: our fellowship, our loyalty to one another, our humanity, our courage, our generosity, the greatness of heart that has grown because of these troubles. When our persecutors come to be judged by you let all these fruits that have been born be their forgiveness."

If a young man who is facing a gas chamber can write that days and hours before his own murder, then surely you and I can forgive one another. Today, let us convert this day of memory of 9/11and those horrendous acts into a day of conversion in our own hearts where we choose to forgive that one person who up to this day, we have not been able to forgive. It is a choice of the heart; it is a choice of the will to forgive; may we forgive in the Lord's name.

The Gospel Joy

The children were having a fun day at the beach: riding the waves, building sandcastles, and playing Frisbee with the dog. In the distance, an old woman appeared. Her tangle of gray hair fluttered in the wind. Her tattered clothes hung on her like old rags bundled around her shoulders. Her incomprehensible muttering buzzed above the sound of the waves. As she walked along, every now and then, she bent down to pick up God-knows-what from the sand and stuff whatever-it-was into her shopping bag.

As the woman approached the family playing in the sand, the parents instinctively moved towards their children quietly instructing them to stay away from the strange woman. As she passed by, she smiled kindly at the children, but the smile was not returned.

After they left the beach, the father asked some of the local folks about the "spooky" old lady on the beach. "Oh, that's Maggie," he was told, "She's a kind old soul. Every morning and afternoon she walks the beach picking up bits of glass or sharp stones and shells so the children won't cut their feet."

We are so quick to judge others by outward appearances. We are so quick to cast people aside by the mere fleeting image of them or having heard them for just a couple of minutes. We have cast a judgment on them, a judgment of the total sum of who they are. We know instinctively that we should not do it, but we continue to do so.

Today's reading from the Gospel is about judgment. It is about the judgment on the final day; it's about how God is always just and always merciful. So merciful that He will allow into the kingdom of heaven even those who come to Him in the very last hour of the very last day of their life. Yes, He welcomes all into the kingdom of heaven, and all we must do is say yes.

But those who were working in the vineyard of life from the beginning of the day seem upset by God's generosity; they seem angry that someone else can have a very-last minute conversion in their life. Inside of us, we say, "That's not fair. I've been good all my life; they only just started a couple of years ago. Why should they get salvation the same as me?" And yet instinctively, we too know that is wrong and we struggle in allowing ourselves to celebrate other people's salvation. The fact is that everyone, every single human being is called to salvation and that all we have to do—all we have to say is, "Yes, Lord. I accept." Then, for the rest of our lives we are called to live that out, to enjoy knowing that we are saved, knowing that we have already realized now what the Lord has promised us for all eternity. The challenge in this Gospel is that because it is a stranger, we find it hard to accept. But if it were one of our own family; if it were one of our brothers or sisters and we knew how they have struggled all their life with addiction, or how much they struggled with being a thief or being in some way down and out, and in the last moments of their life, they were rescued through some miracle, we would celebrate. We would be delighted that they finally have seen it.

Let's do something with today's Gospel. For a moment, pretend that you are one of those workers and that five of your brothers are with you. We are day laborers and we are waiting for someone to hire us. Right away, somebody hires us, but not your brothers. Later on, while we are in the vineyard working away, we look up and see your brothers starting to work later on in the morning. Immediately, we celebrate because we now know that your brothers, who are equally as poor as us, have just now gotten a job and money. When we look at the story in that light, we have no problem celebrating that we all get the same salary because it is my brother who is getting it and we can celebrate because we know he needs it and he is one of us. We are called to believe that we are all one family; the entire human race is one family. So, if somebody who has not come to church in years comes back, we celebrate that gift. If somebody comes who has not been here in years, we should say, "Yes, praise God." Not because of something that we have done but because it is an opportunity for God to bless them. It is an opportunity for us to share the joy of the Gospel. We too can celebrate the joy of the Gospel, knowing that in the end, our death will not be the end, but it will be the beginning of eternal life.

Today, we, who gather regularly at the Eucharist, should celebrate anyone who comes our way, anyone who finds a way to come back to the Lord.

We celebrate it because their salvation and their joy are ours. When we choose to live the Gospel, we choose to live it with a joy-filled heart. But is it always easy to do? No, it is not. And as a matter of fact, it is very hard to do and that is why we come here so often. We come to the table to be nourished and to be strengthened by seeing so many others gathering trying to live out that Gospel, trying to live out that joy. That is why we come here, to be nourished by Christ to go out and be the evangelizers in our world; to be the joy of Christ in our world.

Today, let us not leave here with some sort of mellow heart; may we leave here with joy-filled hearts and may we spread the good news of His Gospel with others and be alive in His spirit. That is the message of Christ. All are welcome at the table. All have been offered salvation. All we have to do is say "Yes" and then live out the Gospel joy.

Mountain of the Lord

These last few weekends, I have had the opportunity to preside over several weddings. It has been a great privilege to do so. One of the great joys for me is to see how the day is full of energy and love. It is such a privilege to stand and watch two people promise and commit to each other for the rest of their lives and to love and honor each other as long as they live. Somewhere in the service, I always try to remind them what they are doing is setting out on a journey as opposed to having arrived at a destination. What they have really done is arrived at the beginning. This is the beginning of the rest of their lives; —the very beginning of an exciting journey. It is "now" when they start to live what they have promised today.

In that sense, it is a bit like taking a journey hiking up a big mountain. When we decide to climb a mountain, we get ready, we set our course, but we have not actually gone anywhere yet. The decision is one thing, but the action is another. When we set out initially, we have no real idea what is ahead of us and in fact, there are days and times in the climb when we go, "Oh, ah, I can't go any further. I just can't do it" and we want to abandon the hike. Somehow, we remain steadfast because we have made the commitment and we want to get up to the top, so we keep persevering

I think that is very much like marriage; you must continuously commit to it. It is very much a continuous, day-after-day endeavor. It is not a once-off commitment that happens on your wedding day only, but instead it is a commitment that you make over and over again every day, to commit to love one another each and every day.

I think that the same metaphor can be used for our own discipleship. In our own Baptism we made that commitment to follow the Lord. We commit to the beginning of a new journey and we set our hearts on doing the Lord's will to reach the mountain of the Lord. But it is the beginning of the journey and there are days when we find it really, really hard and we struggle with it. Sometimes we even want to turn away and walk away from the belief that we can do it. Sometimes it is so hard we say, "Oh, I just can't go on." And yet, if we remain steadfast and we keep climbing the mountain of the Lord, we find ourselves enriched, enriched by the commitment we have fulfilled, enriched by the goal that we have set for ourselves and to which we have remained steadfast. It is that sense of discipleship the Lord is talking about in today's Gospel and first reading. The first reading today is from the Prophet Ezekiel who warns us that it is never too late to start out on the Lord's journey. It is never too late to decide to want to climb the mountain of the Lord. In those ancient times, the people understood that there were those who had sinned and those who were pure if you would. Those who had sinned, or their ancestors who had sinned, believed they were doomed to evil. But those who had good fortune could go on to good things. The Lord is speaking to Ezekiel, saying no, that is not true. It does not make any difference when you turn back to the Lord; "I will forgive you," says the Lord. But it is the turning back, it's the conversion, the setting off to the mountain of the Lord, it is the commitment to decide to go that matters. Sometimes we, as Christians, decide, "Yep. I'm going to be a good Catholic Christian." Somehow, we convince ourselves that the more often we say it, the more we would become that person. However, we must go on that journey. We need to become that good Catholic Christian. There are times when we want to turn around. There are times when we are tired of being that good student at school, tired of always being that one in the family who is the first to forgive. It is those times when it seems that the mountain is just too hard to climb. But the Lord assures us that that is the right journey we are called to, to remain steadfast and to do the Lord's will.

Today's Gospel speaks about the same thing, asking those who have yet to turn to the Lord to turn now. The Lord reminds us that it doesn't make any difference who else starts to climb the mountain. We must climb our own climb. We ourselves must set out and go up the mountain of the Lord. The Scribes and Pharisees felt those who were coming late to the game shouldn't get in, shouldn't get on the mountain or shouldn't be allowed onto the way of the Lord. But the Lord says, "No. All are welcome." We need to not fear about anyone else coming to the Lord because anyone else climbing the mountain should give us joy that there is company on this mountain of the Lord. I do not know where many of you are. Some of you are at total commitment and really are on the mountain of the Lord. You are working hard at it and know exactly what I am talking about. There are others of you that may be struggling with this. You may be at that very point where you are saying, "Oh, I just can't go on. I can't do it anymore. I just can't." I encourage you to remain steadfast to the commitment to discipleship, to remain steadfast to climb that mountain of the Lord and to not give up. There are still others of you that are probably here, but you really are not walking on the mountain. You are here but there is nothing here. You are here only in person and you are really, really struggling and I know that can be very hard but please know you are on the right mountain. It is never too late to turn back and to start climbing. Do not give up on the commitment that you made in your own Baptism. Our role is to work our own journey and to work our own discipleship. Through that discipleship maybe others will see a witness to it and may set out on the mountain themselves. The best thing we can do is to be the best Christians that we can be. May we nourish ourselves at this table with strength for that journey and let us set our hearts once again on that mountain of the Lord.

Pay Back a Portion Out of Joy

Some of us rent the homes we live in; others own the home they live in, or more appropriately what we should say is that they co-own the home with the bank. As we learned from the last financial crisis, most people do not actually own their home outright; most have large mortgages which they pay, and they co-own the house with the bank. They pay their portion to the bank as their portion of the ownership.

In renting a house it would be strange if we were to decide not to pay this month's rent. I would just skip it for a couple of months because I don't really want to pay it. The way mortgage companies act today is quite simple; if we choose not to pay, they will foreclose. And we know how painful that reality is for some of us today.

The reality of our lives is very similar to that reality. We do not really own this body of ours. We think we do, just as we think we own our house. But we are really co-owners with the Lord as this body is the temple of the Holy Spirit. That is what the Lord has called each one of us, a temple, the dwelling place of His spirit, in each one of us. To that end then, we are co-owners with the Lord of even our own bodies and indeed our whole world. Just as it would be absurd for us not to pay our rent or mortgage, it is equally absurd for us not to pay back to the Lord some portion of our lives and the fruit of our labors. Because after all, it is not completely ours.

The financial crisis today brings to bear the fragility of one's financial state. So also, when our body is in illness, the lack of health brings the knowledge of how fragile and vulnerable we are to all sorts of physical, mental or emotional disturbances. Our body can quite easily be attacked in these different ways. But we don't say that about our soul because we believe that when we die, our soul goes on to eternal life. So, in a sense, this body of ours is just a passing place for us. We co-own it with the Lord.

Today's first reading talks about the vineyard of the Lord; how He gives it to somebody to tend, to produce fruit and to then give back a portion, not the whole amount, just a portion back to the Lord. We are called to do that in our own lives. We are called to take what we have been given to work the vineyard, to work our bodies, to produce great things and to do great things in our world. Then we are always called to give back a portion of it to the Lord because it is not ours. We do not do so out of a sense of obligation to some sort of vindictive landlord; we do it because it is the right thing to do and we do so out of gratitude. It is divine righteousness because we are given the gift and we do it out of great joy.

The reason we say "great joy" with great clarity is the fact that the scripture language had special significance and certain images referred to certain realities. For example, in the Old Testament and in the New Testament, the word "bread" was considered daily sustenance. Whenever they used the word "bread" in the stories, it had to do with daily nourishment. However, that is not what Jesus used in today's Gospel. Instead, He used the words "wine" and a "vineyard." Those words were symbolic of the joy of life because people would have a drink of wine in company and it was considered a time when one enjoyed life. Instead of using an example of a field of wheat, He uses a vineyard. In other words, we are given the great joy of life and it should then be a great joy to share a portion to the Lord. Our motivation to share our time and talent comes not out of some sort of obligation, such as in paying our mortgage or rent, nor is it meant to be the motivation of our lives. The motivation is wine which is symbolic of joy. We are called to share what we have because we realize that we have been blessed. There are times when we find it easy to recognize God's presence and there are other times when we find it more difficult to recognize how blessed we have been in our everyday life. But that is where we must start.

We must look at our ordinary daily lives and even during difficult financial struggles, or difficulties in our country and in our world; we still see the presence of our God. We still have our health and we have our children. The point is that we still have the gift that God gives us, which is our very self, and that is our starting point. We give to others from a point of gratitude. We give of our time and we give of our talent and we share it, not just with our family, but we share it with our community. We share it with God because that is what we are called to do out of joy. It is divine righteousness to share whatever we have, a portion, not all of it, a portion back to the Lord.

As we leave here today nourished at His table with bread and wine, recognizing God promises to do both: give us what we need in sustenance with the bread and give us the joy of always being with us with the wine. Today, we go away from here filled both with our daily bread and the joy of life, realizing we need to go and share; share with joy a portion of our time, talent and treasure.

Accepting the Pardon

In 1829, George Wilson, a postal clerk, was part of a plot to rob a federal payroll train. During the robbery, Wilson killed a guard. Subsequently, Wilson was convicted and sentenced to hang. Public sentiment against capital punishment led to a movement to spare Wilson. Three weeks before Wilson was to hang, President Andrew Jackson intervened and granted a Presidential pardon.

But for some unknown reason, Wilson refused to accept the pardon. Wilson's refusal led to a legal conundrum in the court system because they did not know what to do. Could an individual refuse a Presidential pardon? Chief Justice John Marshall handed down the Court's decision: "A Presidential Pardon is a deed, to the validity of which delivery is essential, and delivery is not complete without acceptance. It may then be rejected by the person to whom it is tendered and indeed it would be invalid. If it is rejected, I know of no such power that this court has to force a man to do something that he has refused to do." The pardon was rejected by George Wilson; he was subsequently executed and hanged. A pardon must be accepted for it to be valid.

Our pardon exists, but it needs to be accepted. That is the message that Christ is trying to get across in today's Gospel. He is saying that we have been given pardon and the salvation of eternal life. We are given it as a gift, but we must accept it. And if we do not, then the pardon is not valid. It cannot occur. That may be hard for us to understand, but really, the greatest gift that God has ever given us, is our freedom, the freedom to accept and even the freedom to reject God's love and God's salvation. That is what today's scripture is all about: the ability to be able to accept or reject the gift of salvation.

Now, we are all here today, so I trust that we are all in agreement that we have accepted this offer of pardon and salvation. Okay, so now we say, well that's great; now we're done with the Gospel passage. Uh. Uh. Wait. There is this one little part in the Gospel about a man at the wedding being "without a wedding garment." Now, you might find that very strange. You might say, if you invite them in from the byroads and the streets then you need to accept them even though they are not able to be dressed up. To begin with, we need to understand that at that time, if you did not have a wedding garment of your own, the wedding garments were supplied at the door on your way in. Similarly, if you went into a fancy restaurant today not wearing a jacket, a jacket would be supplied for you to wear.

So, not only would he have arrived without a wedding garment, but he would have deliberately refused to wear the garment offered him at the door. The symbolism for you and me is that we are given the invitation and if we accept the invitation, there are responsibilities that come with that acceptance. There are moral responsibilities to live out with what we claim in our baptism. Because if we don't live them out in everyday life, then baptism is nothing more than an empty ritual. It becomes just water poured over our head meaning nothing to us. Well, that is not what we are called to do. Instead, we come every Sunday to the table to receive the bread and the wine made into the body and blood of Christ. It reminds us of the promises we took in baptism: to always live for Christ and to put Christ first in our lives at all times.

I know that is not easy. And I know sometimes we would like to shed the wedding garment and do what we want in our life, but that is not what we promised. We promised we would live it out and that is why we come here each week. We know that the promise needs nourishment; it needs strength. Now, there are lots of reasons why we would not choose to live the way the Lord has asked us to do by not putting Him first in our life. There are lots of distractions at the office, in school and at home. There are a multitude of tasks that need to happen every day with our children or the things that we want to do.

There are lots of reasons to not put Christ foremost. In today's global economic climate with the turbulent times we live in, there are anxieties and worries inside of us. I understand that those are difficult to deal with. I am not trying to minimize that. But what I am saying is that what the Lord promises us if we choose Him first, if we give back to the Lord first is that all the rest will find a way of falling into place. That does not mean that we give up on doing things; that we don't have to go to work; that we don't have to do anything around the house; that we don't have to take care of our kids or our parents, or that our economic woes will just disappear. None of that is going to happen.

What I am saying is that everything will be made different because we believe that Christ is first and foremost in our life. We choose to put on that wedding garment every day of our life. It requires of us to put on that cloak of love, to put on that cloak of humility, of kindness to others, of gentleness to others, of forgiveness towards others. These are hard things to do. That is why we come to the table to receive nourishment and strength so that together, we can go at it one more time.

Today, we who have accepted the pardon and who have acknowledged the validity of the pardon by our acceptance, have received delivery and now we must own up to the responsibilities of having that pardon. We live out in our lives every day the choice that is Christ. We choose to put Christ first in our life and then put other priorities back behind that. Today, we accept the pardon and reclaim and re-choose Christ.

Church *in* the Modern World

From 1962 to 1964, over 2,700 Bishops from all over the world gathered for the Second Vatican Council. It was a major highlight in Church history and set a new direction for the Church worldwide, promulgating seventeen major documents on Liturgy, ecumenical and interfaith dialogue, religious freedom and social justice among others.

In 1964 the last plenary session the Council produced its final document called "Gaudium et Spes," or in English "The Church in the Modern World." It is one of the most prophetic documents of the Catholic Church. Originally the document was called "The Church *of* the Modern World" as opposed to "The Church *in* the Modern World." Imagine for a minute over 2,700 Bishops argued about a preposition "of" or "in" the modern world.

You might wonder, "Why?" Several hours, thousands of bishops arguing over a preposition. Why? The reason was there is a theological difference between the two words. On one hand we could be perceived as a church "of" the world as in "separate" from the world. On the other hand we could be perceived as a church "in" the world as in being immersed in the world. We are not a church "of the world" as in "from the world" but we are "in the world as part of the world" and our role as a church is to be immersed in the world and to be a voice in the midst of the world.

This is a prophetic stance that is very biblically rooted. We, as a church, are the people of God and we are in the midst of this world and our voice and our witness come from being in and living in the world. This is the point that Christ makes today in the Gospel in response to this rather cynical question about the taxes to Caesar. "Should we pay this tax to Caesar or should we not?" they muse. The answer was not an either/or answer but a both/and. We must pay our taxes and we must give to God. We must be in the world and still be the Church, the living Body of Christ. Fundamentally, our role as Christians is not to keep Christianity alive in the church building here but to live the church in the world out there. Our role is to gather each Sunday around this table to receive the body and blood of Christ and then go out to be the Body and Blood of

Christ to others in the world. We are not separate of the world; we are part of the world and our role is to be alive in the world.

Our role, as Jesus says in today's reading, is both the civic responsibility to the state and the moral responsibility to God of being church. For example, when it is time to vote, Christ says it is our responsibility to be a good citizen and vote whatever way our conscience tells us to vote. But it also our responsibility to know what the Church teaches, and we are called to be that role in the world too. The church teaches that our vote needs to count in the world, whatever that vote is for any of us. Our responsibility comes straight from scripture.

But it does not just stop there; our responsibility of being a church in the world is about caring for others in the world. We do that primarily through our family and friends but also to all people in our community. Our role as Christians is about being church to others, about reaching out for what we call in the church the "common good," not just for all Catholics but for all people everywhere. Our role is to do the right thing for the right reason because it is good for all in the society. Indeed, our role is to always care for the weakest first. That is what the Church teaches us to do in the midst of our world.

We have an example of that here today, because after the baptisms today we will anoint those who are looking for prayers of healing, those who are seeking anointing of the sick. The sick among us will come forward and in the name of the church, we will ask God to give them special blessing giving them healing and strength through this sacrament. But more importantly, for these new families, who now welcome their children into the church, we promise to be witnesses to them by our presence here today; we promise to be witnesses to them of the loving presence of Christ in this world; they will look to you and me, not just to their moms and dads, but to you and me as to how to be that living presence in the world.

We need to be honest and admit that it is hard work. It is really hard work because there are times when we just don't feel like being nice. There are times when we just don't want to be the good person anymore and just do what we want to do. Instead the Gospel calls us to a moral responsibility of being a light in the midst of a darkened world. We are often surrounded by people like those in the Gospel today who asked

Jesus a cynical question. But we don't give in to that cynicism. Instead, we lay claim to our responsibility of being the bright light of this world, to ensure that all in this world, Catholic and non-Catholic will believe in a God who is good, a God of love and a God of hope.

That is our role as Christians. We come to be the light in this world, to always seek and to do the common good. We are reminded each and every Sunday what we celebrate here is being Church together and then we leave here to be the "Church *in* the Modern World."

The Garden of Our Hearts

As many of you know, I love to go hiking or walking each morning. These last months, I have not had an opportunity to walk in the neighborhood but instead I have been hiking in the hills. Last week, I had the opportunity to walk in the neighborhood again and I noticed a difference. I recognized the homes and gardens that people take care of and those that people don't take care of as well. There are two homes I noticed that have changed in these last several months. One home was recently purchased about 6 months ago. The family moved in and put great energy and commitment into the garden. They tore out the old shrubbery and dead bushes and each weekend, slowly and methodically, they did a little bit more. First, they tilled the soil then built up a small wall, a dividing wall between the pathways. Next, they put down a new sprinkler system. Slowly they put in vegetation: new plants, new trees, and even some new fruit trees. Then they built up some rockery, even a fountain. Slowly the garden took shape. It is now becoming absolutely spectacular as everything blossoms and everything comes into full maturity.

On another part of my walk, I see another garden that has also recently changed owners. It is a rental and obviously they don't care too much. It used to have a beautiful green lawn, fruit trees and gorgeous flowers that blossomed along the front pathway. In these last months, it is so sad to see how it has deteriorated. It is no longer a lush garden. The grass is burned, flowers are dead and even the beautiful fruit tree in the garden is dying.

The difference between these gardens is not so much the beauty of the garden but it is the commitment to making these gardens what they are. On the one hand, we have the commitment of a family that goes out each weekend and tills the soil, plants and then reaps the benefits. On the other hand, we have neglect. They do little or nothing, leaving the plants to rot and die.

I think this garden analogy serves us very well today as we listen to the Gospel. Consider that the garden of our lives is a garden not for ourselves but a garden for others. In today's Gospel, Jesus reminds us that the greatest commandment of all is to love God with all our heart, all our soul and with all our mind and to love our neighbor as ourselves. This biblical love is not so much affection as it is a commitment to serve. In other words, this garden of our lives which we must till is not so much affection for others as it is a commitment to serve others.

The garden of our lives is not just about putting up a wall and maybe some nice grass and flowers to look at but to plant fruit trees, like that wonderful neighbor. The fruit of those trees is not only for us, but also for the benefit for others. Who are these others? Who are these neighbors we are called to serve? We are reminded of that today in the first reading from the book of Exodus. Those we are called to serve and take care of are not only our family and friends which are considered a natural obligation, but over and above that, as a community, we are called to reach out to those who are least able to take care of themselves. In today's readings those would have been the widows, orphans and the poor, the migrant or foreigners who have no one to take care of them. You and I have been privileged with many gifts from God. We are called to plant fruit in our gardens, fruit trees of all sorts so that others will benefit from them. So, what does that really mean in our own lives? It means we are called to be generous and not just to look inward but to plant in the garden of our lives fruit trees for others. That fruit tree is to listen and care for others who are in trouble. Maybe we may not feel affection for them, or even like them, but we are committed to serving them because love is a commitment to others and we are called to commit ourselves to serving others.

Today and every day, we are called to serve God by serving others. It is not easy and that is why we come to this table each Sunday, to receive that strength, and to go at it again. Indeed, it is hard work, but surely, we look around here today and we recognize so many others, who are willing to till the soil of their lives, to pull out the weeds and to plant new plants. It is not always easy, but it does help to look around the neighborhood, to see what other people have done with their lives so that we can flourish together and to make our neighborhood and the fruit of our trees free fruit for others.

Today, we leave here, nourished and replenished at this table of our Lord. As Paul says to the Thessalonians, we come to teach the catechism by the way in which we live our lives. We teach others by the way in which people view our lives, by the way we come to be charitable, to be kind, to be humble, but above all else, to love our neighbor as ourselves. If we do this, then we know we love God from our heart, from our soul and from our mind.

Cheering Us On

One of the great mysteries of our Catholic Church, and most misunderstood outside the Catholic Church is our whole devotion to the Saints and in particular to this Feast Day of All Saints. They do not understand why we pray to the Saints for intercession. They do not understand why we hold them up in any way. They think we should pray to Jesus Christ only because He is our God and our savior. In one sense they are right, Jesus Christ is our savior and our God. We should, and we do, pray to Him.

But one of the things that the saints do for us is they give us models of how to be a Christian. We believe that the Lord calls every one of us to be a saint in God. Every one of us is called to be that saint. But we hold up certain people who have done very well in this life, people who have had extraordinary ways or maybe have just done the ordinary things in extraordinary ways.

Yet, so we are clear, the saints are a motley group. I want to be honest with you. They are not your ordinary folks and they are from every way of life. There are some saints who are young and there are also some saints who are old. There are people who have worked in the professional world; there are people who have never held a job. There are men, there are women, there are boys and girls and there are saints from every kind of place. Part of the reason why the church has, in its wisdom, held up all these saints is because there is bound to be somebody we can identify with. There is bound to be somebody that we can look at and say, "Wow, look at that. I can do that!" Unfortunately, in today's world we do not hold up our saints as our models. We do not seem to study the saints like we used to or talk about the saints like we used to. Who would you say is your hero? Who do you say you want to be like? We all have a slightly different way that we look at people and we like them for this reason or that reason. Sometimes we like them for their achievements their courage or abilities. And sometimes it is because of their success in sports or entertainment. There are a lot of different reasons we find ourselves looking up to them.

We believe the saints are people who we can hold up as models of how to be. Now as I said, they are all different and every one of us will end up with different saints. Look for a saint that you can identify with, maybe St. Therese, who only lived to the age of twenty-four, a young person. Maybe St. Francis, St. Thomas or St. Peter and the list goes on. I have some of my favorite saints who celebrate their feast day this month. Part of the reason is that there is something about them that we can identify with and then we live our lives holding them up. We look up to these people to admire them and to follow not necessarily their exact example but to say look, here are ordinary people and they did extraordinarily well with the ordinary gifts.

Every single one of the saints started out as a child just like you and I. Every single one of them just did the ordinary things with extraordinary love. That is all they did. They did not set out to be venerated as saints all over the world. What they did was love Christ with all their heart, with all their mind and with all their soul. And they did the simple things. St. Francis loved the earth; he loved just doing the ordinary things, things like serving the poor. He did not make it any more complicated than that. He just said I want nothing more to do than to serve the poor and hold onto them. St. John of the Cross, one of my favorite saints, only wanted to be a pure and simple priest. So, he got rid of all the other stuff in his life and he focused on that alone. There are many ways to live out our discipleship. We are called to do the ordinary things in our daily life. Ordinary things that we are good at and to find out what is that one thing that we are very good at doing and then doing it well for Christ. You see in the scripture today that is exactly what He calls us to do. He says blessed are the people that do this. Blessed are those that come and follow him. So, I ask you to find one of the saints and to pray to them. Not that we pray to them instead of praying to God, but we pray to them as friends and we say help me to live this life, help me to be a good person. That is the way of our saints. They are cheering us on, helping us and encouraging us on our way. One of the biggest parts of our belief in the Communion of Saints is that they are still alive. We believe that when we die, we do not disappear. We become one with God and we believe that those saints who have gone on before us, those who have died, are now with God. So, in a very special way they are very much still with us. There are saints that we know by name but there are also other saints in our lives who are un-named, people we knew to be holy. It might be a grandmother or a grandfather, it might be an uncle or an aunt who died or it might even be a mom or dad who has died. They were very special people to us, and they were holy to us. They are still with us cheering us on.

Look for one of the saints and call them by their name and ask them to help you in your daily life. I could not imagine my faith without the saints. They are as close to me as God himself. Whether it is those big saints I know by name or those little saints like my father, they cheer me on and help me on my journey. These are the people we are called to model our lives after. Today, let us be in communion with those saints and ask for their help to do God's will.

Thin Places

In ancient Celtic spirituality, we believe that our ancestors and those who have gone before us in our faith are very close to us; their spirits remain with us, never quite that far away. We even have a word for the female spirit called a Banshee. When it is a cold and wintry night, we can even hear the Banshees howling in the wind. It is not meant to be a scary reality, but a comforting reality: that our ancestors are never quite far away; that they surround us like a warm wind on a cold, winter's night. They are always there to protect us from harm, always there to ease our anxiety, always there to encourage us in life's struggles.

There are certain times and spaces that are more significant than others. We call these places "thin places." We call them thin places because we believe that the divine comes so close to the human that we can almost taste it; we can feel the breath of God right among us.

Some thin places are events, others are places and others are gatherings. One such thin place is that of a funeral. When people gather for a funeral, we believe that the souls of all the faithfully departed come to pick up the one who has died so that they can be with the saints and God. There is a particular sacredness to that space of the funeral. Indeed, that is why in Ireland the funeral is such a big occasion for the community because another true thin place opens in the community.

We also believe that there are mountain tops, or places like meadows which can be thin places. In Ireland, they are often called places of pilgrimage. One such mountain top is Croagh Patrick. Many a person has climbed up in pilgrimage to the top of that mountain and has experienced that same reality of sanctity at the top of that hill.

We also consider every church to be a sacred place, a thin place, where God's presence comes close. But most especially, we regard the sacraments as thin places. At this very table, we believe the Lord comes ever so close, so thin a place, that we can feel His presence and experience His complete essence among us. Indeed, as Catholics we believe that He is literally in the Body and Blood of Christ, not just a thin place but a divine space.

Today and in these last few days, we celebrate All Saints and All Souls. They are not meant to be a scary reality. We recall all the faithfully departed, not because we are afraid of them, but indeed because we want them to surround us like a warm breeze on a cold night. We want them, their presence, to be ever with us and we want to know that they are now with God. So that is what we hear in today's reading from the Book of Wisdom. That the just are now with God. They have nothing to fear; no torment shall ever touch them. We believe that our faithfully departed have now received the ultimate gift of eternal life in the presence of God. This is what the Gospel refers to today, that eternal life is offered to us all.

But the reality is that we often still miss our loved ones; especially if it has only happened recently. We want their presence—more than just their spiritual presence; we would like to see their physical presence back with us. But we must remember that they are now with the Lord and that their spiritual presence, that very holy presence in the thin places in our own lives becomes a reality because they are with God. That is our faith. We have certainty in our faith that we believe the faithfully departed are with God. We believe in the Gospel today where the Lord takes all to himself; "He will not lose any that were given to Him by the Father." So somehow the Lord will find a way to bring even those less faithful ones to Himself. Somehow in all eternity, the Lord will find a way.

But our part for today, as we gather here, is to realize and listen carefully to the Gospel – that eternal life is available to all of us. We celebrate this thin place here, right here in this Eucharist, the presence of Christ among us and in us. We come to celebrate that with great joy in our hearts, knowing that eternal life awaits every one of us. That our visit to this thin place each week somehow transforms us with the joy of the Gospel. The message we hear today is not a sad message. It is not in any way a sorrowful message. It is a message of joy. Eternal life awaits all of us.

As we join in the celebration here today, as we come to celebrate this thin place and receive the grace of God, we come to be transformed in the world and to transform the world. Today, may we remember all our faithfully departed, all those who have gone before us in the faith, but not with sadness but with great joy in our heart. May we remember them and now go forth from this thin place enlivened by the joy of the Gospel, enlivened that we know we will have eternal life. But for now, we must convince all those around us with the way we live the Gospel, by the way we proclaim it in our actions, that we believe, that we truly believe in the Gospel and the good news of eternal life. So today, we celebrate this thin place, we visit God; God has come among us and we come away transformed to live it once more.

Thirty-First Sunday of Ordinary Time
Malachi 1:14—2:2, 8-10; Psalm 131; 1 Thessalonians 2:7b-9, 13; Matthew 23:1-12

Not How We Look but How We Act

There is a story of a man who was hired at Apple Inc., while Steve Jobs was still alive. He got one of these large offices at the corner of the building and was very proud of his new position. He was hired lower down in the organization but felt very pumped-up about his new office and wanted to come across as important. He was in his new office sorting out all his stuff when he sees one of the maintenance staff at his door. He quickly picks up the phone and says, "Uh-huh, yes Steve. Yes Steve, uh-huh, I will, yes, yes, thank you Steve. Thank you for your trust in me, I will do that," and he hangs up. Then he gently looks at the door and says, "Come on in" to the man waiting in the doorway. The maintenance man walks in and says, "Sorry Sir, I'm here to install your phone line." *For everyone who exalts himself will be humbled, but the one who humbles himself will be exalted. Luke 14:11 NAB*

Sometimes we are so caught up in trying to impress people that we forget that it is rather shallow. And most times, even if we are not caught like that, it falls flat and people are not really that impressed anyway. We are so caught-up in how we appear that we spend too much time focusing on the outside and we forget that our intentions on the inside are more important.

In the ancient times the people were also caught up in this. The Pharisees and the scribes were very much caught up in it. The Pharisees and the scribes were good people, at least they were trying to be good people. Their understanding of the law was to take it and to live the law by every single letter of the law. In other words, it is not enough just to do good, we must have the intention of doing what we believe is the right thing in our heart not just to be seen doing good. To that end we want to be careful not to fall into the fallacy of how the Pharisees and the scribes saw their God. They looked at their God as a lawgiver and the people were the law keepers. He was like a spy satellite in their personal world checking and scoping out every little thing they did and marking it down for evidence in the court of life. Jesus came along to say yes, there is the law. He was not saying there is no law. He says that it is

156

not the law that is wrong, it is the interpretation. We must learn to do the right thing for the right reasons. We should not see our God as a lawgiver and we as the law keepers. Instead our image of God should be as our parent and we are the child. Because of that relationship we love our God and we want to do what is right because that is what our parent would want us to do. We love our parent and we know that he loves us. The image that Paul gives in the beginning of his letter to the Thessalonians is that of a nursing mother, a beautiful image. The nursing mother cares and dotes on the child and makes sure that this child has every need met. That is the image of our God which is a very different image from the image of God as judge and lawgiver. This is the relationship we are called into.

We are called into a covenantal relationship and not a contractual relationship. The distinction is that a contractual one is based upon the law, what you did or what you did not do. A covenantal relationship says that you are in relationship with me and we have a commitment to one another, to love one another inside this commitment. It says that God promises to love us no matter what. There is nothing that can separate us from the love of God. No matter what sin we do and no matter how far we stray there is nothing that can separate us from the love of God. We really believe that our loving relationship with our God is that He will always love us.

The example He gives us today is the loving parent. There is pretty much nothing we can do to separate ourselves from the love of our mother or father. I think there are a lot of things that we do that separate us, but I think that the mother's and the father's instinctual love is to love no matter how hurtful or broken their child becomes. No matter what they say or do that hurts, parents cannot help themselves but continue to love them. That is what the Lord says to us. He will love us no matter what. It is from that point that we are called to go forth and love one another.

We are called because we have been given this love and we are called to share that love with others. Then we go out and we do acts of kindness and justice in God's name because we were loved first and we understood this love from God. It is the reason why we forgive somebody in our family or our friends who have hurt us. It is the covenantal relationship with our God that we are called to keep.

There is a wonderful book called the "Primacy of Love" that talks about the practice of virtue. This book starts and centers all the other virtues around the virtue of love. If we do not have the virtue of love then all the other virtues become empty. We must practice the virtue of love first and foremost and then everything else is built around that. Then the law is fulfilled through the way we live our lives. It is hard work to always love others. We know there will be times when we fail but we will not give up trying. It is the journey of loving one another we are called to take up.

Today, once again, let us recommit ourselves at the Table of the Lord to that lifelong project of loving one another in that covenantal relationship that God gives us. It is the single commandment that He gives us to love one another and in so doing we love our God.

Be Prepared, Be People of Prayer

My soul is thirsting for you my God. Several weeks ago, all the priests of the Diocese were on retreat with the former Archbishop of San Francisco, Archbishop John Quinn. In many of his sessions he spoke of several of the saints and called us to a deeper prayer life. One saint he referred to several times and really focused on a lot was St. John of the Cross. I had read a lot about St. John of the Cross' writings in the seminary and I really loved them. He's considered one of the mystics of the sixteenth Century. He was a wonderful profound spiritual master and a prolific writer. Archbishop Quinn challenged us back to a stronger interior life. I was very interested, and I recalled my own passion for that in the seminary. I have been reading St. John of the Cross every day since and was drawn back into his writings and it has been a spectacular journey.

One of the core teachings of St. John of the Cross is that all created life has a center. There is a center within them that is created by God. Yet there are different centers like concentric circles. All created life has some center; even inanimate objects. But a human being is made in a different way, with *"profundo centro"* as he says in his native Spanish or "profound center" in English. In this space there alone God speaks to us in our heart. As human beings on a journey of life and faith, we are called to seek and to find that *profundo centro.*

We need to become aware of that interior center of ourselves for that is where God gives us the wisdom for life. It is that draw towards the interior life that the author of the first reading today was referring to. He uses the analogy of wisdom being a beautiful woman and the lure of a woman one could not possibly resist. He is trying to say that wisdom is so beautiful and so amazing that you cannot *not want* to have that wisdom. There is a sense of urgency about attending to the wisdom within. It is the same way St. John of the Cross refers to wisdom as irresistible. We are drawn into ourselves and yearn for our divine spark within us. If only we could just spend some moments reflecting on it. That wisdom is available to every single one of us in that *profundo centro* within us. In the Gospel today Jesus tells us that we are called to prepare to receive wisdom, much like the author of the Book of Wisdom. This is not a passive preparedness or passive waiting but an active waiting where we prepare well. It is similar when we prepare to go somewhere on a trip. We do not passively prepare. We prepare by thinking through what we will need on the trip, how many days we will be away and then get all our stuff ready. This time of preparation is quite busy. When the time comes to go, it is almost a relief because you have done all the preparation and now it is time to go on the trip. The Lord is trying to tell us that we must be actively preparing for this moment, and not passively waiting so that when we are called, we will know the Lord because we have prepared and are ready.

I know you have heard me say time and time again, the only way I know that we can prepare is by being people of prayer. We need to learn how to seek that *profundo centro* within ourselves. There is no other way. Unless we spend some time alone with our God being quiet and still, recognizing the *profundo centro* where God alone speaks to us, we will not be prepared. I think that sometimes we are like people who have cataracts in our eyes. We cannot see because there is something blocking us. It is as if we cannot see that interior reality of our lives, so we seek to get that outside. There is that yearning of the soul, our soul is thirsting for God but we seek to fill it out there somewhere, sometimes in not so good places. Instead we are called to be still and be quiet removing the cataracts of our heart and spending time with God.

St. John of the Cross would say that there is no substitute, that we must do it, as he says, in *soledad*, in solitude. That does not mean loneliness, but it does mean we must retreat from the busyness of our lives and the word he uses to describe that is *templanza* which is temperance. There is lots of stuff we could do, there are lots of places we could be, but we need to temper our lives and spend some time in *soledad*, in solitude, with our God. In that moment we need to be still in the Lord's presence and to listen to his wisdom with our own heart.

Try and spend ten minutes minimally each day alone with the Lord seeking and finding that *profundo centro* in your life. I promise you that any minutes you spend in prayer each day will be given back to you thirty, sixty, a hundred fold in the wisdom and the patience and the kindness you will receive in those few moments in quietness and stillness with the Lord. I know it is hard with our busy lives, but I know of no other way to overcome the difficulties of our lives. When we seek and find that *profundo centro* within ourselves, the darkest night is never dark, the worst pain is never bad enough that we cannot get through it, the hardest loss is never too much to overcome when we know our God is inside with us each and every day. It is like a light that burns within our own heart that no darkness can ever overcome. That light is within every single one of us but we must be willing to spend some time in *soledad y templanza*, in solitude and temperance seeking and finding the God of wisdom, the God who is Christ, the God who is within us in the *profundo centro* of our lives.

Who's Got Talent?

I am not sure if you have ever seen any of those TV shows of the "Got Talent" series, *America's Got Talent* or *Britain's Got Talent*. It is basically about finding undiscovered talent. They do auditions and eventually end up before a panel of three or four judges in front of a live audience in the studio and on TV. The audience in the studio and at home votes on who has the best talent.

Every now and then, they discover somebody who is an absolute surprise. It happened last year in the *Britain's Got Talent* program when a middle-aged woman, plainly dressed, shyly went on stage and the judges asked, "What do you plan to sing?" She replied nervously: "I am going to sing *I Dreamed a Dream* from the play Les Miserables." For those of you who do not know this song, it is very beautiful but very difficult to sing. As soon as she said this, the judges sort of elbowed one another and started giggling publicly. The camera panned to the audience and everyone was nudging each other, some even laughing before she had opened her mouth, snickering at this woman and what she was going to sing. Then she sang.

From the first word that came out of her mouth, there was just stunned awe in the entire audience in the studio and those watching it at home. She had an absolute magnificent operatic voice. Since then, Susan Boyle has gone on to such great heights still maintaining her brusque unique character. What was amazing about that evening is that everyone, even those of us at home, had judged Susan Boyle by the way she looked. We had cast a judgment before she said a single word. We all did it to a certain degree. Some of us might not admit it but we all did it. Most of us were expecting her to make a fool of herself and instead she made fools of us.

We are so quick to judge one another by what we see on the outside. We cast people into categories, and we expect them to fulfill that category even though the evidence is often different. We continue to keep them in those categories, and we do not recognize what their talents are and we most certainly don't encourage them.

In today's Gospel, Jesus is speaking about the gifts from God. Everything we have is a gift from God. Yet we often fail to see the gifts in others and even in ourselves. We tend to judge before we see or experience others. We often do not realize what God has already given us. It is only when they are gone that we realize the gifts that we have. Do we understand how blessed we really are? It seems we are so consumed with wanting more and more. We never seem to ever have enough. We want what somebody else has. We don't want the gifts that we have; we want the gifts that somebody else has. We don't realize how gifted we already are.

I do not know at what point enough will be enough. When are we going to be happy and truly content with what we have now? Can we see how we are blessed with family and friends; the person sitting next to you as a spouse, or a child or a brother or a sister or even just a friend? Do we realize how blessed we are right now before we ask for anything more?

God has already blessed us, and I don't know why it is we cannot see that. We get so caught up in little things like the petty arguments that we as families can sometimes have. They can consume us so much that we forget the love that we share and the amazing gifts that we have. Yet we fight over the silliest little things and I just don't know why. We hold onto grudges that go on for years sometimes. Why? We have been blessed with so much.

In today's Gospel, there is a sense of urgency in this understanding. This isn't like, "Oh, if you get some time, and you realize how blessed you are, then attend to those gifts." There was a real urgency to it. Do it Now! Because we don't know the time or the hour! We don't know when our last minute could be, so we ought to live now and be grateful now with the talents and gifts that God has given us. We need to do something with them and share them with others.

What is very important in today's scripture is to realize that the person who got five talents and the person who got two talents got the exact same reward. "Well done my good and faithful servant. You have done well with these small responsibilities. Now I will give you great responsibilities. Come share your Master's joy." It was the exact same response to two different gifts. It is a reminder that God measures us not on how much we have returned to Him but on how well we have done with what we have been given.

St. John of the Cross puts it a little more beautifully and eloquently. "In the evening of our life, we will be judged not on how well we have lived but on how well we have loved." So, my friends, in the end, what we have been given is not what matters. It is what we do with what we have been given that matters. We have all been blessed abundantly and we do not need anything more. We need to use those talents to the best of our abilities and if we do that then we will hear those words: "Come my good and faithful servant; come share in your master's joy."

In the end my friends we will not be judged on how much we have lived but on how well we have loved. Let us love well and live in Christ's abundance.

Final Test

When I attended university back in Ireland, almost all our classes were graded on the final test alone. In other words, it was 100% — everything rode on that final exam, 100% of your grade was typically on just that test. Now, two things happen as a result of that: one, you work really hard for that test and you get very good at cramming and the other is that you get inclined to be a little bit lazy throughout the year because you sort of skirt along until the final exam.

You can imagine my shock when I came to the United States and attended university to find out there was a different system of grading; especially when I got to the final exam and they told me it was not 100% of the grade. So, I said, "Well what is it?". My friends told me that the final is only part of the grade and most of the grade is on "continuous assessment" of all the little tests throughout the year. I said, "Oh, they count? Oh. Oh." So also does class participation. The grading system is usually about 40% on the final exam and 30% of your grade on class participation as well as 30% on the continuous assessment in tests. As a result of this grading system, you must remain more engaged in the whole class because you are being tested all along.

In today's Gospel, we hear about what we have traditionally called the final judgment; it's a bit like the final test. It might be a bit of a shock to those who figured out our final test is not based on the Irish university system but more on the American university system. In other words, we get tested not on the final words we say, but on the continuous assessment of how well we have done all our life, especially as Jesus says "how we treat the little ones." None of us knows for sure how the final judgment will occur, but scripture tells us time and time again and Christ reminds us time and time again that God will judge us not on what we say but on what we believe and what we do. Like any good teacher I'm sure God will consider any unusual circumstances or difficulties that were not our fault. However, we know through Jesus' words, God has no time for lazy servants who choose not to live the words because they are hard and inconvenient to do so. In other words, it is our actions that count much more than our words. And in particular how we treat the little ones, the ones who are least able to take care of themselves. Jesus gives us a very colorful analogy today. It is the illustration of a shepherd separating the sheep from the goats. Now we must be honest, none of us are all pure sheep and none of us are all pure goats. But if we are honest with ourselves, we know that there is a little bit of a sheep and goat in all of us. We want to be less goat and more sheep. We want to be able to always be looking to follow the Lord, but we know there are times we do things and say things that are not in line with what the Lord would have us do or say. So, what are some of those things? Today's scripture talks about what the continuous assessment is based on. It is based on, if I can summarize, to "Feed the hungry:" to feed the hungry who hunger for food; to feed the hungry who hunger for water, for clothing, for company, for love, for tender care because they are in prison or because they are sick. They are hungry for spiritual nourishment or physical nourishment, or emotional nourishment. We do not get to judge why they are hungry even if that might sometimes upset us. We are also called to work for justice to prevent them from being hungry again whether that be spiritual or physical hunger. We are called to feed the hungry. That is our mission as a Church.

As our own individual mission, we need to reflect on how we spend our time, talent and treasure in our stewardship. I don't know about you, but I always work better when I have a goal. Some sort of plan that helps me get to where I want to go. I may not make it the whole way, but I intended to do this, and that is where I am going. This should be our goal: to make a commitment to the Lord and His church that we will do what He has asked us to do. And so, we need a plan on how we will achieve that goal. How will we spend our time, talent and treasure in service to the Lord in the continuous assessment of our life? What commitment will we make to the Lord, to our church and parish community?

Once we make a plan or goal towards this end, we need to hold ourselves accountable to that plan.

Why? Well, today's Gospel tells us why. Because it is the continuous assessment! Today, we don't want to be the lazy servants and decide not to do it because it is just not convenient. Instead, we want to be the good and faithful servant, to get ourselves involved in this risky business that we call the mission of the church, to commit ourselves to feed the hungry.

Because we know that in the end of our time, we will be judged not on what we say but on what we do.